Lucille Rosengarten, ACSW

Social Work in Geriatric Home Health Care
The Blending of Traditional Practice with Cooperative Strategies

Pre-publication
REVIEWS,
COMMENTARIES,
EVALUATIONS . . .

"**T**his book is actually three books in one—a detailed description of clinical social work interventions with dependent elders and their families; a manual for establishing a cooperative home health care agency; and a guide to training, supervision, and team building of paraprofessionals. The difficulties inherent in balancing the needs of clients and staff are frankly addressed. Abundant examples of conflicts encountered and resolved in daily practice are presented as works in progress. The authorial voice is a fresh one—raising important questions, suggesting creative strategies, honest in admitting problems, and uncompromising in the search for solutions that respect the abilities of each staff member as well as the uniqueness of each client. Everyone interested in the future of home care will find much of value here."

Ann Burack-Weiss, DSW
Adjunct Associate Professor,
Columbia University
School of Social Work,
New York, NY

More pre-publication
REVIEWS, COMMENTARIES, EVALUATIONS . . .

"**L**ucille Rosengarten has given us a gracefully written book on geriatric home care based on her pioneering efforts to bring cooperative home care to the United States after discovering its development in Bologna, Italy, nearly twenty years ago. Through detailed written case studies, Rosengarten reveals how a committed social work practitioner can honor the wishes of the elderly for independence and dignity as they weather severe chronic ailments and life-threatening illnesses. Cooperative social work services in the United States face an uphill battle in a culture suffused with ideas of competition and privatization. Fortunately, Rosengarten gives practical advice to start up cooperative structures and to create humanistic patterns of interaction between social workers, home care providers, the elderly, and their kin. The author personifies the ideal of the practitioner-scholar with high ideals and practical solutions."

George S. Getzel, DSW
*Professor, Hunter College
School of Social Work,
New York, NY*

"**L**ucy Rosengarten has articulated well a subject rarely discussed in social sciences—the tension between competition and cooperation. We teach our children both values, and affiliate with people who provide the greatest comfort level along the spectrum from fierce competition to loyal cooperation. Add to this broth values from other cultures, along with dependence on help from outside the family circle during vulnerable episodes late in life, and the stage is set for heightened conflict.

Despite these constraints, Lucy Rosengarten shows in her clearly written book the rewards and potential of cooperativism in home care with the elderly. In particular, she highlights the need for different training techniques, and feedback from home care workers *and* clients.

Of particular interest is the team approach between nurses and social workers, and the sensitively described involvement of the clients in ongoing decision making about their care. Though often promulgated in social science literature, in practice, especially in the home care field, cooperative planning, working, and training is rare. Lucy Rosengarten provides practical guidance for the aging and housing network to move in this direction. The elderly will benefit and so will we when we join their ranks."

Friedhilde Milburn, CSW
*Executive Director, James Lenox
House Association, Inc.;
President, Health Advocates
for Older People, Inc.*

Social Work in Geriatric Home Health Care
The Blending of Traditional Practice with Cooperative Strategies

HAWORTH SOCIAL WORK IN HEALTH CARE
Gary Rosenberg and Andrew Weissman
Editors

A Guide to Creative Group Programming in the Psychiatric Day Hospital by Lois E. Passi

Social Work in Geriatric Home Health Care: The Blending of Traditional Practice with Cooperative Strategies by Lucille Rosengarten

Social Work in Geriatric Home Health Care

The Blending of Traditional Practice with Cooperative Strategies

Lucille Rosengarten, ACSW

The Haworth Press
New York • London • Oxford

The Haworth Press, Inc., 10 Alice Street, Binghamton, NY 13904-1580

Cover design by Jennifer M. Gaska.

Library of Congress Cataloging-in-Publication Data

Rosengarten, Lucille.
  Social work in geriatric home health care : the blending of traditional practice with cooperative strategies / Lucille Rosengarten.
      p.   cm.
  Includes bibliographical references and index.
  ISBN 0-7890-0746-0 (alk. paper).—ISBN 0-7890-0747-9 (pbk. : alk. paper).
    1. Aged—Home care—United States. 2. Frail elderly—Home care—United States. 3. Social work with the aged—United States. 4. Medical social work—United States. I. Title.
HV1461.R65 1999
362.6—dc21
                                                                                   99-29261
                                                                                        CIP

CONTENTS

ABOUT THE AUTHOR

Lucy Rosengarten, ACSW, BCD, is Founder and Executive Manager of Concerned Home Managers for the Elderly, COHME, Inc., and is a member of the Social Work Faculty of The Mount Sinai School of Medicine. She has taught case management and cooperativism in various academic and community settings, and her articles have appeared in leading social work and nursing journals.

Before founding COHME fifteen years ago, Ms. Rosengarten worked for ten years as Mount Sinai Hospital's first social worker in their home health care department. She developed the social work role there, working collaboratively with many medical and social disciplines both within the hospital and the outside community. She handled complicated floor discharge planning throughout the hospital and aimed at returning frail and sick elderly safely to their homes, rather than to nursing homes. She has made thousands of counseling home visits throughout New York City.

Acknowledgments

I am indebted to my husband, Frank Rosengarten for his contribution to our year's research in Bologna (1981-1982), which is reflected in his co-authorship of Chapter 6. I am also grateful to him for his editorial expertise and for the many thoughtful exchanges I have had with him concerning the issues dealt with throughout this book. His constant support and commitment to this project were indispensable to me.

I would also like to thank my supervisors and colleagues at the Mount Sinai Medical Center, some of whom taught me the basic principles of home care social work, while others encouraged me as I explored a somewhat untraditional path toward cooperative and comprehensive geriatric case management. They are Claire Bennett, Florence Bernstein, Helen Blakes, Susan Blumenfield, Barbara Brenner, Sylvia Clarke, Hannah Lipsky, Jan Paneth, Helen Rehr, Gary Rosenberg, Lois Schein, Penny Schwartz, and Andy Weissman.

Other social workers and nurses who have influenced my thinking a great deal throughout my twenty-five years in the field are: Carole Bahou, Ann Burack-Weiss, Suzannah Chandler, Rose Dobrof, George Getzel, Rea Kahn, Barbara Keyes, Charlotte Kirschner, Friedhilde Milburn, Janet Petterson, Maura Ryan, Emma Shulman, and Trudy Smith.

Ann Berson read the manuscript with the same sensitivity and insight she showed in her previous editorial work with me.

COHME's Board of Directors, administrative staff, and aides continue to struggle steadfastly with me to realize the potential of our collaborative approach to geriatric home health care.

Foreword

What you are about to read in *Social Work in Geriatric Home Health Care* is how a professional social worker drew on traditional social work values, knowledge, and skills to create a new model of home health care for the sick and frail elderly in the city of New York. Shifting from long-term nursing care, which dominates the field for this population, the author develops a marketplace, a consumer-responsive cooperative agency of services. Rosengarten combines her experiences in a medical setting and in its certified home health agency and her year-long observation of an Italian home care cooperative, into a democratic, staff-run fee-for-service licensed home health agency that has been in operation for fifteen years. Although the social worker and nurse hold key roles in social and health needs assessment of clients and families, it is the emphasis on personal assistance and that group of aides who provide the major service in the home that make this book valuable. The aides are as critical as the professionals in assessment and planning.

The value of the text is that the author repeatedly demonstrates social work skills—individual and family focused, sensitivity in counseling (even adopting a filial-type stance where she encounters "aloneness"), involvement of an informal or formal network as needed, investment of a known community, and an ongoing relationship with a team of other health care professionals. However, two dimensions are the mainstay of this private fee-based service: the staff that provides personal assistance to the agency's clients (with their developed sensitivity to observed need and services), and the nurse and social worker home visits that underpin physical and psychosocial planning.

Rosengarten draws on cases in most of the chapters and she clearly demonstrates social work counseling not only with the primary client, but with as many members of the informal network who should be and can be supportive in a caregiving role. For example, when aloneness and infirmity are factors in the case of a frail, single woman, the social worker moves into a "filial" role and facilitates transfer to a formal structured community-based social worker.

Throughout, one feels the author's strong conviction to treat the ill elderly in a family context, drawing on informal and formal supports, comprehensive in focus with the collaboration of other health care and social work providers, and with full awareness of community resources. Her observations of the "at home" clientele led her to develop an innovative and unique support group. These patients and their spouses as mutual-aid-givers meet in their own home environments, sharing experiences and developing friendships. The creation of support groups among homebound, frail elderly and their spouses or adult children is a unique program started by Rosengarten. Having seen the benefits of this program, she is concerned with how to get formal social home health programs to go beyond one-on-one services.

In Part II the author reflects on her observations of the Bologna, Italy home health care system and the interviews she conducted there, which became the underpinning for Concerned Home Managers for the Elderly (COHME). The progressive policies, the cooperative founded on democratic interchange among all staff—professionals and aides—in decision-making, became the prototype for the fee-for-service geriatric home health agency she created. Training and decent economic support of the aides gives them status in a self-management program. Rosengarten describes setting up COHME as a non-profit health care agency with decision-shared responsibilities, within policies and procedures that conform with state regulatory bodies. She writes about the problems encountered in developing cooperativism among staff members, illustrating these with her experiences. The seven tenets that she prescribes for COHME are outlined and essentially describe the partnership among all staff in carrying out the agency's mission.

Part III will prove helpful to those who want to set up a geriatric home health agency because here she offers her training and supervisory experiences. She moves from one-on-one supervision to group sharing training and discussion of experiences sessions. Rosengarten's use of examples and illustrations make this a "how-to" book, as she offers concrete approaches to working with aides facing difficult situations. The vignettes, as core content, serve as informative orientation and as the introduction of recognized principles in caring, for example, confidentiality and compassion. In this section Rosengarten touches on the sensitive topic of white/black relationships and discusses how to develop a "trust" factor between the client and the aide where ethnic differences exist.

Part IV restates the development of COHME, adding the dimension of contracting on behalf of a Medicaid clientele with municipal agencies, along with the continuance of privately paying clientele. COHME is a "living laboratory" of a geriatric home health agency for the sick and frail elderly "to test what works and doesn't work." Principles of case management are emphasized that Rosengarten believes can best be implemented by trained social workers as the professional case managers. The conclusion lists existing problems in developing sound case management programs in today's underfunded marketplace for "at home" services.

In this volume, which is written in a personal style, Rosengarten is totally social work oriented as a team-based case manager. She clearly supports an "at home" model of care versus residential long term care. She projects the encouragement of local social service agencies to develop their own fee-based personal care programs and also Medicaid-supported programs to enable more frail elderly and functionally disabled persons to remain living at home. Rosengarten sees these programs with a social work value, knowledge, and skills base and the social worker as case manager. The model she has developed is responsive to the needs of consumers of long-term (and even short-term) care, providing a supportive environment for consumers of the service, while giving an enhanced status to home aides in a democratically run agency. Her model will serve as a blueprint for the future of geriatric home health care agencies.

Helen Rehr, DSW, ACSW
Professor of Community Medicine Emerita (Social Work)
Mount Sinai Medical Center and School
City University of New York
New York City

Introduction

This book is an account of my experiences and insights from the time I was hired in 1974 as the first home care social worker at Mount Sinai Hospital in New York City, up to my recent writings in the 1990s that deal with Concerned Home Managers for the Elderly (COHME), a nonprofit, licensed home health care agency that I founded in New York City in 1985. My ten years at Mount Sinai had consolidated my belief in the necessity of comprehensive social work case management to keep frail elderly safely at home. It was at COHME that I was able to move my thinking forward in this area.

COHME derived its basic principles from a cooperatively managed home care agency in Bologna, Italy, where cooperativism and various progressive social programs have been prominent features of daily life since the end of World War II. It was in Bologna, during a year's leave of absence in 1981 to 1982, that I was first introduced to consciously organized cooperative methods of providing home health care for the elderly. Subsequently, in 1984, I met Rick Surpin, who was laying the groundwork for Cooperative Home Care Associates (CHCA) in the South Bronx. In our discussions we recognized that, although we shared many views on workplace democracy, his ideas grew out of community organization, while mine developed within the framework of social work as part of hospital-based home health care. For this reason, we took separate paths. I think, however, that the existence of both CHCA and COHME is testimony to the practicality of cooperative methods in home care.

A significant number of chapters in this book describe the ways in which I have struggled, together with my co-workers, not only to improve conditions for our workers, but also, mainly through the use of the One-Sheet, to advance the state of the art of social work geriatric case management. The One-Sheet is a unique COHME-created instrument that distills the case assessments and plans in a readily accessible format.

These struggles, I believe, hold some valuable lessons for the future of home care in the United States, especially now at the turn of a new century when so many aspects of the health care system under managed care are undergoing change at a disconcertingly rapid pace. Amid this change it seems to me that the accomplishments and even some of the setbacks of COHME provide useful examples for geriatric social work practice throughout the United States.

Among the themes of the early chapters in Part I that I think are of interest to both professional and general readers are the roles played in effective home care by informal community-based networks and the problems and needs of caregivers in their efforts to help their ill spouses.

In Parts II, III, and IV, I would like to single out the following topics for the reader's attention: The first is that of the home care aides themselves, without whose devoted and intelligent service to the geriatric patient no other aspect of home health care can even begin to be effective. The quality of training, ongoing education, and daily work life of the COHME aides constitute one of the two primary concerns of COHME, which, in addition to providing excellent long-term care for its clients, strives as part of the agency's mission statement "to offer our employees work that is meaningful and fulfilling." Some of the ideas and practices described mainly in Parts II and III document what I think are innovative techniques and methods for enhancing the dignity of home care work as a service vital to sick elderly clients and their families as well as to the larger communities to which they belong.

Second, in Part IV especially, this book explores many crucial areas of case management, whose effectiveness, when cooperative strategies are employed, depends not only on the skills of a single authoritative social worker with the ability to oversee and coordinate all aspects of a given case, but also on the extent to which all members of the home care agency assume responsibility for their special tasks as they relate to the overall management of a given case. In other words, unlike traditional home health care agencies, where hierarchical structure and specialization of tasks are paramount, COHME's case management requires a high level of interaction among aides, office staff, nurses, and social workers, all of whom share their expertise with the overall case management team coordinator (CMTC), who in turn is responsible to fellow workers, to the doctors who care for the patient, and often to the referral source.

Among the problem areas of case management covered in Part IV are (1) the challenges of creating effective One-Sheets for each home visit (i.e., concise one-page reports that include the precipitating event, identifying information, assessment, and plan) and (2) the provision of ongoing counseling that fits the specific circumstances as described in the One-Sheet. Special emphasis is placed on the importance of involving the client in the management of his or her own home health care.

Third, this book faces some of the practical issues that inevitably confront all home health care agencies, but especially those that might prefer to utilize cooperative strategies. One such issue is dealing with state regulatory authorities, where the general trend in home health care has been away from an emphasis on social work in caring for the sick elderly and toward privileging the nursing function. It is much easier to measure nursing tasks in a precise empirical manner than the quality and quantity of social work functions. Excellent nursing care is essential in home care, yet too often quantitative criteria of evaluation are looked on with such favor by policymakers in state and federal governments that social work tends to be relegated to secondary importance.

Another issue that COHME has faced involves internal conflicts that ensue when, as a result of a certain degree of business success, the agency needs to pay very careful attention to financial and administrative problems while striving at the same time to remain true to its original mission and to its cooperative leanings.*

---

*Several years ago, it became necessary for COHME to require its Board of Directors to become much more intimately involved in the agency's daily activities than was the first Board of Advisors that carried out limited oversight functions in the early years of the agency's history. Suffice it to say here that the COHME Board of Directors, while in agreement with the agency's mission and mode of work-life, nonetheless is constantly alert to the "bottom line" and to a whole range of other business concerns. The resulting tensions within the board itself and between the board and the agency workers on all levels are a positive element as long as they can be resolved without sacrificing basic principles.

Finally, it is necessary to mention the problem of educating not so much the home care aides, many of whom come from countries where cooperativism is an accepted value, but the office workers, the nurses, and the administrative personnel, for whom vertical, authoritarian, and hierarchical structures, although not always welcome, are nonetheless familiar and preferred by them to what they see as the loosely defined vagaries of democratic workplace organization. Their complaints are numerous and often valid, since cooperativism at a single small agency cannot offset the enormous influence of the larger political climate in which they live, where centralized and top-down decision making is regarded as the best way to run a successful business.

COHME represents a different way of organizing home health care for the sick and frail elderly in New York City at a time when the percentage of people over sixty-five who will require it is rapidly increasing. I hope that this book will serve as a social work contribution to the ongoing debate among home health care workers and legislators about the direction in which geriatric health care should move at the turn of the century.

PART I: HINTS OF A NEW KIND OF CASE MANAGEMENT IN TRADITIONAL HOSPITAL-BASED HOME HEALTH CARE

The five articles that make up Part I are case studies of how my cooperative leanings began to emerge some twenty years ago in the course of my work in traditional geriatric case management as a member of the home health care department of Mount Sinai Hospital in New York City. What I brought to my job at Sinai was a commitment to group work together with a sensitivity to the importance of all the players in the formal and informal support systems. Prior to beginning this job, I had already acquired a commitment to group work through earlier volunteer community activities. This commitment was then focused and professionalized by my graduate social work training. Furthermore, as I gained expertise in the home health care field, I noticed that I was frequently activating or creating more groups than seemed usual in this type of social work, to the benefit, I thought, of my patients and their families. At the same time I noticed that active home care social workers rarely conceptualized their practice and were not writing sorely needed articles about their case management skills in a manner that would let legislators and other health care workers know how critical their social work role was to maintaining seniors safely at home. As a result of this experience, I became determined to write up my work.

As a case manager, I began to emphasize and strengthen groups that already existed and then moved on to create many more of them. I began to realize that I had extended these groups into patient activities that could not be supported within a traditional home care agency, due to agency constraints. I needed to consider the possibility that there was another way to organize home care and that with research, study, and a lot of help, I might be able to start a new kind of home care agency.

Chapter 1

The Dying Marriage Counselor: A Poor Family in Crisis

My first meeting with Mrs. Sims, an eighty-six-year-old black, extremely frail woman with advanced bladder cancer, occurred unexpectedly when the home care coordinating nurse rushed into my Mount Sinai office and asked that I immediately accompany her to the emergency room. There Mrs. Sims lay on the examining table, quietly crying, with her eyes tightly closed. Surrounding her were her sixty-year-old nephew, Mr. Reese, and her cousin, Mrs. Jones. Mr. Reese was screaming that regardless of the doctor's decision, he would not take Mrs. Sims home again. He wanted her admitted and had even brought her luggage with him. He could not keep her at home. There was too much to be done for her, no doctor would come to his Harlem apartment, he was ill himself, and his wife refused to help. As Mr. Reese stormed out of the emergency room, the home care nurse and emergency room nurses calmed Mrs. Sims and began preparing her for examination. I walked with the cousin, Mrs. Jones, into an adjoining room.

Mrs. Jones stated that Mr. Reese had "reached the end of his rope." His marital situation was indeed very poor. There were constant arguments, which upset Mrs. Sims greatly. Mrs. Jones stressed that Mrs. Sims must be admitted to the hospital for her well-being and for the sanity of the whole family. When we returned to the examining room, Mrs. Sims sadly stated how much she wanted to stay in the hospital. Since there would be further delay before the doctor's examination, Mrs. Jones agreed to remain

This chapter was presented at the Thanatology Symposium, Columbia University, titled "Home Health Care and the Quality of Work," April 21, 1976.

with Mrs. Sims. I told both I would look for Mr. Reese and see Mrs. Sims tomorrow, wherever she was.

I could not find Mr. Reese around the emergency room area and returned to my office. As I approached, I heard Mr. Reese screaming at the home care director and secretary. I brought him into my office, where he banged my desk, reiterating his demand that I see that Mrs. Sims be admitted.

As I commented, "You're having a tough time, Mr. Reese!" he burst into convulsive tears. He related his misery and frustration at not being able to care for his beloved aunt, who had raised him and had taken him and his family in when he had been "down on his luck." His wife had recently been planning to become a nurse's aide, but she hated Mr. Reese so much now that she would not help him with Mrs. Sims' care. Also, he had an old back injury that caused him great pain. He just could not think straight anymore because of his physical and emotional stress. Here indeed was a man in crisis!

I spent time helping Mr. Reese ventilate his strong feelings, while we awaited word from the emergency room doctor about whether Mrs. Sims could be admitted. Mr. Reese calmed considerably and felt that he could now return to his aunt's side to await the verdict. I restated to him the promise I had made to Mrs. Sims in the emergency room—that I would see both him and his aunt tomorrow, wherever they were, and would continue working with them to plan for the best future placement for Mrs. Sims. I would also be available to help the family with their intense anxiety and domestic conflict related to Mrs. Sims' illness.

The next day I learned that Mrs. Sims had not been admitted. Home care had arranged ambulance service to return Mrs. Sims to her home. I called a remarkably calm Mr. Reese and arranged my home visit for later that morning.

I arrived to find Mr. Reese in robe and apron preparing breakfast for Mrs. Sims, who, he pleasantly reported, was sleeping. He said that the doctors had changed her medications, the pain had lessened, and she had a comfortable night. His back, however, still bothered him a lot and he had to move around slowly. I took note that the three-bedroom apartment was comfortably furnished but untidy. Mr. Reese appeared to enjoy his culinary role and boasted he had been a cook in the army. As our conversation continued, Mr. Reese's mood ranged from calm rationality through sadness and then angry withdrawal, as he respectively discussed his care of his aunt, his concern about his aunt's death, and finally his wife, whom he said he would like to divorce. He and Mrs. Sims had helped her all through their thirty-year marriage and had recently supported her plans to become a nurse's aide. Now, his wife had deserted them both. Mr. Reese became suddenly silent. I suggested that he join me as I interviewed his aunt. He quickly snapped out of his withdrawal and offhandedly stated that after he served his aunt breakfast, he planned to take a bath. Mr. Reese's behavior vacillated between that of a responsible adult and that of a child.

I entered the bedroom alone. The room appeared adequately set up as a sickroom with a telephone nearby. (Mrs. Reese's work?) I saw a full urine bag lying on the floor; there were unpleasant odors and general littering. Mrs. Sims greeted me weakly, and said she'd been awake and had heard my conversation with Mr. Reese, and was very saddened by it. As she began to cry, Mr. Reese breezily brought in what I felt was a nutritionally inadequate tray of food. He reminded Mrs. Sims to take her medications and hobbled out of her room and into the bathroom, where we heard, from behind the closed door, the shower running and happy whistling. Mrs. Sims noticed that I was looking at the room's clutter. She remarked that she knew her nephew was not taking good care of her, nor was his wife, but of course, Mr. Reese had his bad back and there were all those marital problems. She felt that she was the cause of the quarrels, and she was helpless to change things. This knowledge seemed to increase her pain. She had been so disappointed the previous day when the hospital did not admit her. "Couldn't you get me into a 'special hospital' until I am strong again and can help my family?" asked Mrs. Sims. Now she was crying again. I realized that she either did not know her diagnosis or was denying it. I told Mrs. Sims I would certainly do all I could to improve her situation. I asked what she understood was wrong with her. She stated she had had a tumor removed from her bladder and been "X-rayed" to prevent its return. The X rays had burned her inside and made her weak. If she had only refused the X rays, she would be well today. I asked if she had ever discussed these beliefs with her doctor. She said that the doctors kept changing, and they were all too busy to listen to her at the hospital. She used to have a nice doctor who came to see her at home, but he had been mugged and refused to come again. That is why they came down to the emergency room whenever her pain became too intense.

Apparently exhausted from this outpouring, Mrs. Sims closed her eyes and moved deeper into her pillow. She began to speak of happy family moments of the past, when she had been well and actively helping her nephew and other family members—physically, emotionally, and financially. She confided that her nephew had always been "different"—immature, erratic, and in constant need of her guidance. She had helped raise him in the South and had brought him North with her. She always kept an eye on him, even after she married. She had never been blessed, she said, with any children of her own, but she felt like a mother to everyone—family and friends alike—and they in turn sought her out continually for advice and counseling. Widowed and penniless in her mid-fifties, Mrs. Sims had determined she would not depend on family charity. She found a position "downtown" as a live-in governess. She set up this apartment for herself for her days off, vacation times, and most important, to provide a home for her nephew. She was away too much, she said, and "Junior," as she called him, began to "stray." Mrs. Sims knew a "nice girl" and she helped arrange things so that the girl and Mr. Reese married. Mrs. Reese always expected and received Mrs. Sims' full support. Mrs. Sims observed that this girl could not now be expected to handle a full load of family responsibilities, especially her illness. It was no wonder she had bolted and run, but it was very hard for Mrs. Sims and Mr. Reese now.

I asked Mrs. Sims if she felt a part-time homemaker, paid by Medicare through our home care department, might be of immediate help, while we continued to consider the special hospital she had mentioned, as well as her domestic problems. She stated that she would appreciate such help greatly. We discussed her neighbors and church members who had offered assistance. I encouraged Mrs. Sims to contact them now, in order to reactivate her community support network.

I then asked how her nephew's marriage had been before she became ill. She said she now realized they had not gotten along well for a long time, but while she had been working, she had not been aware of how bad things really were between them. I suggested that this would mean that her illness did not cause the marital conflicts. She felt that her illness did not help matters, and it was clear from her nephew's behavior that he wanted her out. I said that I felt her nephew had shown mixed feelings about her, but perhaps we could all talk about this together at my next visit the following day. She hesitantly agreed.

After this initial interview, I assessed that Mrs. Sims was struggling with dual needs—to be cared for during this critical stage of her illness and to be strongly in control of family affairs—most particularly, the present marital crisis of her beloved nephew. If she could be assured that home care, family, and friends would see that she was as physically and emotionally comfortable as possible, she would be able to once again actively participate in her family's daily problems. She could have a meaningful life within the limits of her terminal illness.

Also, I felt Mr. Reese had an opportunity to use this crisis situation to improve his emotional relationship with both his wife and his aunt. At age sixty, he still displayed many adolescent attitudes and needed to be helped to become more independent, to separate from his surrogate mother, and perhaps even begin to take on Mrs. Sims' decision-making role in the family.

My initial plan was to strengthen Mrs. Sims to resume her matriarchal, counseling role and to use myself as Mrs. Sims' "consultant" to help her strengthen her nephew to carry on for her after her death.

The home care nurse arranged for frequent visiting nurse services and immediate placement of a home health aide. The urology resident who had examined Mrs. Sims in the hospital reported to me that she would probably only live one or two months more. In a staff meeting, we determined that Mrs. Sims could be maintained at home, with maximum home care support. I felt that an alternative plan must be begun, in case the home situation deteriorated and because Mrs. Sims had expressly asked about a special hospital. I therefore sent application forms to a terminal care facility near Mrs. Sims' family.

At our second home interview the following afternoon, Mr. Reese was dressed and in better spirits, having seen the doctor about his back problem and having been impressed by the immediate improvement in his aunt's care with the home health aide's arrival early that morning. Mr. Reese said that if all his days were like today, he would have no problem keeping his aunt with him. I asked about his wife. She had not come home the night before, which apparently was not unusual, and Mr. Reese stated he enjoyed not having her "aggravating ways" around. He gave me an impish grin, asking how I had "hexed" his aunt, since she had insisted he put another chair in the room before I came and that he be dressed before my arrival. Before I could answer, he took my arm and gallantly guided me into Mrs. Sims' bedroom, then turned and walked away to the kitchen, where he had "a date with tonight's dinner." He walked with far less difficulty now—away from a difficult meeting!

Mrs. Sims' room was now very tidy and there were no unpleasant odors. Mrs. Sims herself looked refreshed and was lying on a comfortable sheepskin. She reached for my hand and thanked me for the home health aide. Still, she continued to think a special hospital might be better. I said I had begun paperwork for such a hospital, but it could be easily withdrawn if she decided to stay home. She said she still felt her nephew did not really want her, although he did seem cheerier today. I suggested we ask him as we had planned the previous day.

Mrs. Sims vigorously rang a bell, newly placed by her bedside, and Mr. Reese appeared with a white towel over his arm, saying, "You rang, Madam?" We laughed as Mrs. Sims motioned him to sit in the newly available chair. He sat smilingly by her, patting her hand.

Mrs. S: Now stop the foolishness, Junior, we've got important plans to make and you've got to settle down and listen and give us some serious answers. Tell me right out, in front of this lady. Do you really want me here—this sick and all?

Mr. R: Sure I do, Auntie, but I wasn't good enough to do it all before.

Mrs. S: Well, now the hospital's home care's here, and Mrs. Johnson next door said she'd fill in. With you, and your kids occasionally, and the church ladies, I'll have all the help and company I'll need. But there's a much bigger problem—you and Laurette. I don't want to break up your marriage.

Mr. R: Look, Auntie, it was never any good! Why won't you believe that? I don't want her anymore! I don't even want her in the house, upsetting us all!

Mrs. S: Well, you don't have to get so huffy about it! I'll stay awhile and we'll see how things go. Marriage is a sacred thing, remember that!

I continued tri-weekly visits. Further medical problems were relayed by the aide, visiting nurse, or myself to the home care coordinating nurse, who contacted the appropriate clinic doctors, who were able to provide medication and advice by phone. My interviews were varied—sometimes with Mrs. Sims alone, sometimes Mr. Reese alone (once he let me help prepare a sauce), sometimes the three of us, sometimes with the aide. Although I heard that friends and family members were helpful, Mrs. Sims apparently scheduled their visits not to conflict with mine, and I never met any other family member or friend. I often felt that Mrs. Sims did not want my competition when she "held court"!

During our first few interviews, I encouraged Mrs. Sims to reminisce about her past successful life. I facilitated communication between Mrs. Sims and Mr. Reese around a variety of family concerns. We made very little progress about the divorce issue, each unable to hear the other's views of this matter. I had more success in helping both cope with their anxieties about Mrs. Sims' increased physical weakness and occasional bouts of intense pain.

As Mrs. Sims became progressively weaker, physically, her mental energies grew. She told me she had started doing "this marriage counseling business" without me (but maybe I was her role model, I thought), because Mr. Reese needed Mrs. Reese to care for him "later." She would not amplify this statement, but continued to tell me that she had managed to get both Mr. and Mrs. Reese to sit together with her in this room without screaming all the time, so she must be making headway. She was obviously proud of her work and it was her primary interest.

Later that week, Mr. Reese talked to me in the kitchen while his aunt watched a favorite television program. He said that his aunt's constant "bugging" him about getting back with Laurette was getting him down. All her talk about marriage being sacred and his needing Laurette to take care of him was "driving him up the wall." I asked him why he had not felt able to tell his aunt how strongly he felt about this, at least when I was around. He stated that he did not want to be disrespectful; her dying wishes were of concern to him, and to contradict her might worsen her condition. "But my God!" he began to cry, "I just don't need *her* to take care of me anymore."

I gently asked who "her" was, and it became very clear to both Mr. Reese and myself that the "her" to whom he directed his anger was Mrs. Sims, not his wife, for whom he no longer felt any emotion. This treasured aunt had prevented him from becoming a strong, mature man. She had solved all problems, made all decisions, and had even picked out his wife for him! She had disciplined his children and provided his family with food and lodgings. What was he? What had he ever accomplished?

I said that although I agreed that his aunt had erred in some of her behavior toward him, there must have been something inside him that wanted this treatment up to now. Now it looked as if they both were heading in the same direction. His aunt's primary interest now was that he be able to manage after her death. If she knew that this could be better accomplished without Laurette, and Mr. Reese continued to show the interest in family concerns that he had in our recent joint interviews, Mrs. Sims would probably go along with the idea of divorce and even relinquish her role as head of household to him. Mr. Reese said he would think about what I had said.

During the fifth week of my visits, Mr. Reese began to dress rather dapperly. He spoke of his new social life, his improved physical condition, his renewed relationship with his children, and finally, of his first visit to a divorce lawyer. I looked quickly at Mrs. Sims, who was smiling at me. She told me that she and her nephew had talked it over a lot and this was the right way. Her Robert (not "Junior") was a man now and knew what he wanted. They began to discuss plans for selling some property Mrs. Sims had down South. Mr. Reese appeared to understand and was very involved.

The next week, while in my office, the emergency room notified me that Mrs. Sims was there. I met her with her nephew and cousin, who asked if they could hand deliver the current medical report to Calvary Hospital, the terminal care facility, and take her there right away. I was confused by the request and walked over to see Mrs. Sims, who said that she was constantly in pain and very tired now. She was ready to die now that her nephew and her family were doing well. She just wanted to end her pain and sleep. Her faith was strong; God was with her. She wanted to go to the special hospital.

Since I had made previous application, we were able to arrange for an immediate bed in Calvary. I met Mr. Reese there two days later, sitting at his sleeping aunt's bedside. He asked if we had done the right thing. Should we have continued trying to keep her at home until the end? I suggested he ask his aunt during her brief waking periods.

Mr. Reese called me the next day to tell me his aunt had told him her work was done on earth and Calvary was a good place to wait for Heaven. She died peacefully in her sleep two weeks later.

Although my initial plan was to work with a dying Mrs. Sims to restore her to her matriarchal role, the work quickly enlarged to dealing with the interaction of a family unit in crisis. Mr. Reese's marriage was dissolving. The dramatic situation of his aunt's dying was bringing his hidden lifelong feelings of rage and resentment toward her tyranny to the surface along with his genuine concern for her welfare. He had been her obedient, docile child, and now as he gathered the strength to break away from the marriage that his aunt had prearranged, he collided with Mrs. Sims' need to maintain her strong family position. Mrs. Sims also knew she had to find a successor to her family role and was trying as best she could to preserve Mr. Reese's family unit to provide this stability. I saw Mr. Reese and Mrs. Sims separately and as a family unit. I supported Mr. Reese's ego strengths, working with his adult, not his adolescent, qualities. I helped him to be more honest with his aunt without his taking away too much of her control. I eased his anger, guilt, and ambivalence and enabled him to assert himself with her, to show that he could manage without his wife and could be more responsible in family matters.

Mrs. Sims needed to be kept physically comfortable, and I aided the home care staff in these efforts. I tried to help her with appropriate action within her life process. My original casework goal of helping her maintain her image and dignity continued to operate and expanded to helping her see that there were alternative ways to achieve her desire for greater family harmony. In my family interviews there was little explicit movement toward her becoming more accepting of Mr. Reese's desired divorce, but Mrs. Sims observed my behavior intently throughout these sessions; I became her role model. She learned how to better help her nephew when I was not around and was able to choose to accept his solution to achieve family stability and to trust his ability to responsibly hold the family together.

Here, as is often the case in terminal illness, the greater crisis to be dealt with is the family's interactional process more than the individual's personal reaction to dying. The home environment facilitates such successful crisis intervention.

Looking back at this experience twenty-two years later, I realize that my work with the hospital home care team and the various groups in the community were vital to the success of my interventions. As soon as I made my first home visit and called the hospital, the team there immediately put in a visiting nurse and a home health aide. The doctors in the emergency room had made her immediately comfortable and continued their involvement, at least by phone.

As far as the community was concerned, members of Mrs. Sims' church congregation and apartment house neighbors resumed their previous involvement with her, partly due to my efforts and partly due to her own reactivation of this powerful support network.

These were among the "hints" of cooperativism in my earliest social work cases.

Chapter 2

The Overwhelmed Attorney: A Wealthy Family in Crisis

Mr. and Mrs. Ames lived in a luxury duplex apartment. Mr. Ames, age seventy-three, was a successful attorney who, in his busy daily practice, advised and gave emotional strength to many distraught individuals. Mrs. Ames, age seventy, was admitted to Mount Sinai Hospital with the diagnosis of cerebral vascular accident (CVA), or stroke. This illness left her without normal speech and without the ability to walk or to perform any other activity of daily living without constant assistance. The couple had one child, a married daughter who lived in northern New Jersey with her engineer husband and two teenage children.

The home care nurse first noticed Mrs. Ames lying quietly in her hospital bed, two days before her planned discharge. Mr. Ames was sitting meekly by his wife's bedside, totally overwhelmed by her medical condition and by the prospect of caring for his wife at home. He was barely able to listen to the home care nurse's explanation of the variety of home services we would be providing his wife: visiting nurse, physical therapy, speech therapy, occupational therapy, and my social work services. Later that day, this sensitive home care nurse reported Mr. Ames' upset emotional state to me. We agreed that my home visits would be helpful to this family, not only to assess Mrs. Ames' emotional adjustment to this devastating illness, but, equally important to both the patient and her family, to help Mr. Ames cope with the impact of the return home of his newly stricken wife.

This chapter first appeared in a more extended form in *Social Work in Health Care,* 2(3), Spring 1977, pp. 311-317.

Shortly after his wife's hospital discharge, I called Mr. Ames at his home. He said that he and his wife would welcome my visit the following day. We decided I would arrive at 4:00 p.m. and see his wife. He would join us at 4:30 for a family interview.

Arriving for my initial home visit, I was questioned at the door by a lady in a white dress, who then cautiously admitted me into a spacious apartment. I assumed she was an exceptionally vigilant aide. Having read my hospital identification badge, the aide appeared reassured of my legitimacy but then firmly informed me that Mrs. Ames was asleep and could not be disturbed. I said I had arranged this visit with Mr. Ames and, although I understood her desire to protect her patient, I needed to see Mrs. Ames now. I walked into Mrs. Ames' bedroom and introduced myself to an emaciated woman, lying wide awake in the darkened room, her face turned to the wall. At the sound of my voice, she turned her head toward me, and began thrashing about in her bed, shrieking, grimacing, glaring angrily at me, and finally vigorously pointing for me to leave the room. I was stunned, having received no prior reports of such behavior.

"She wants you out! Only she and me get along good!" said the aide sharply. Indeed, as the aide stroked Mrs. Ames' hair, she became calm. After two more unsuccessful attempts to get Mrs. Ames' attention, I walked out into the living room with the aide. I began to discuss the situation with her, planning to enlist her as an ally in finding ways to establish a trusting relationship with Mrs. Ames. The aide was pleased that I was aware of her calming effect on the patient and began to give me some of Mrs. Ames' history. Mrs. Ames had apparently been quite isolated and erratic in her behavior long before the stroke. At present, she slept through the nights and, therefore, the twelve-hour night aide had few problems; however, during the day aide's twelve-hour shift, Mrs. Ames was fully awake. She frequently became agitated and could only be managed by this aide. The aide went on to condemn the various therapists coming into the home as useless and upsetting to her patient. She said that I had already seen for myself the futility of my own efforts.

At that moment, Mr. Ames returned from work and joined us, as we had previously planned. He reiterated the aide's statements of the impossibility of maintaining his wife at home without her services. Suddenly, Mrs. Ames shrieked from her bedroom and the aide ran to her.

Mr. Ames led me into the living room, sat down, and began to talk to me about the difficulties of the past week. He had to be strong for everyone now, both at work and at home, and he could not keep up the pace! He spoke of his marriage before his wife's stroke. He had accepted the limitations created by his wife's past emotional problems. The duplex apartment gave him an area of the house "off-limits" to his wife, where he could do his fulfilling work and where he found escape from household tensions. Although he recognized the bizarre nature of their relationship, he had been content, and even now he wanted to continue to maintain his wife at home. However, her present angry lashing out and her shrieking upset him greatly. "Thank heavens," he said, "that this sainted aide can handle her!"

I agreed that the aide was amazing and that Mrs. Ames' shrieks had indeed ended. We heard the aide quietly speaking to the patient in the bedroom. Mr. Ames stated that the aide had been a clerk in his law office. One day, she had overheard him telling a colleague that he felt no regular nurse would put up with his wife. She had offered her help. Mr. Ames, grateful and relieved, quickly engaged her. She was quite expensive, did not clean the house, did not listen to him, and he really was not very fond of her, but all that mattered was that she could control his wife.

The aide reentered the room with her hat and coat on, prepared to leave for the day. She had a smug grin on her face. Mr. Ames complimented her on calming his wife. She looked at me and said that she had told Mrs. Ames that if she did not quiet down, she would send me in again!

I was outraged by this inappropriate comment but determined that it would not be helpful to Mr. Ames to react openly to the aide at this moment. Mr. Ames' night aide had called in, stating that she would be delayed on this particular evening, and Mr. Ames was now "in charge" and very anxious. He spoke of his daughter and how much he missed her. Since Mrs. Ames' return home, her wild behavior had frightened her daughter, and now neither the daughter, nor her husband, nor their two teenage children were visiting.

Mrs. Ames missed them too. Their doctor saw no medical reason for Mrs. Ames' strange behavior and was tentatively recommending psychiatric institutionalization for her.

At this point I felt both Mr. Ames and I had to stop in order to sort out and review the problems presented thus far. We placed them in the following order of priority for our future work together—our contract:

1. Problems with the aide
2. Mrs. Ames' violent behavior
3. Mr. Ames' own emotional stress
4. Lack of involvement of children and grandchildren

I asked a now completely overwhelmed Mr. Ames why he had felt no agency had services able to help him manage his wife. He did not answer. I told him that I knew of several reputable agencies with highly qualified personnel, who would do just what his doctor and he felt was needed for his wife. He sat in absolute bewilderment, finally saying: "Just tell me what to do."

Since Mr. Ames needed to be "given to" at this stage in our relationship, I wrote down a list of several agencies, suggesting he call them in the morning. He said that he would test a new aide out this weekend when the present aide was off, since he would not want to give up this aide without some guarantee of an adequate replacement. I then said that I would like us both to return to his wife's bedroom and include her in our planning for the aide replacement. Mr. Ames became even more nervous, fearing his wife's anger for his wanting to change aides. I said that he could tell his wife it was my idea. From our past interview, she could not think much worse of me.

Mr. Ames walked ahead of me into the bedroom and took his wife's hand. When she spied me, she again shrieked and pointed to the door, but Mr. Ames told his wife in blunt terms that I, the social worker here, wanted the aide "out!", that I thought that this aide was not qualified, and that I had insisted he call an agency to get a real aide in the house. I inwardly cringed as Mrs. Ames grunted and motioned for me to come near to her. She began crying convulsively and pressed my hand to her cheek. I began to see that, rather than objecting, the patient was grateful that the aide would be dismissed.

As I began to interview her, Mrs. Ames was able nonverbally to have her husband and me understand that she had really been under the aide's tyrannical rule this past week and that she was terrified of her. Home care reports later showed that the aide had been successful in turning away many other professional visits that week. The aide was discharged and a new aide hired the next day from the resources I had given Mr. Ames. All other home care professionals—visiting nurse, physical therapist, speech therapist, and occupational therapist—were reinstituted, visiting from one to three times a week.

My plan then became to work supportively with the new aide and with Mr. Ames. I made weekly home visits, spending the first half of the session with Mrs. Ames and the aide, role-modeling and teaching the aide ways of working patiently with Mrs. Ames. The second half hour was a family interview, including Mr. Ames. Mrs. Ames' behavior became more controlled and her anger subsided. By my fifth home visit, Mrs. Ames, smiling, dressed, and well-groomed, greeted me at the door. She walked with minimal assistance from her aide to the dining room table. We three had developed a nonverbal means of communication. We used picture albums, magazines, and "yes and no cards" provided by the occupational therapist. The aide gave me information about Mrs. Ames' past week of activities, with Mrs. Ames responding appropriately.

Mr. Ames returned from work for the second half of the session and joined us at the table as usual. At this visit he threw a calendar angrily down on the table. He complained that his wife had kept him up most of the previous night. She kept pointing at the calendar dates and crying. If he didn't get adequate rest, he stated, how could he work? Also, who were all these therapists coming in? He did not know what they did, what their goals were. Didn't he have a right to be kept up to date on these things? I saw these complaints as evidence that both Mr. and Mrs. Ames were becoming emotionally stronger and wanted more control, more power over their home environment.

First, I showed Mrs. Ames the calendar, and then the three of us asked simple yes or no questions about various dates. After thirty minutes of patient work, we learned that Mrs. Ames wanted to know the family's Christmas schedule, including the grandchildren's vacation dates; Mr. Ames' scheduled trip to California; and the new aide's days off for the holidays. Mr. Ames filled in the schedule and suggested that the aide post it where Mrs. Ames could read it easily. This was the first evidence I had seen of his taking control of the household. I then suggested a sign-in sheet for all therapists, with room for their comments. Mr. Ames immediately prepared such a sheet, which he placed in the hall. He stated that he would call his physician the next day for a progress report.

Wanting to support Mr. Ames' now rapidly developing desire to participate in his wife's care, I called the home care nurse and we set up a conference at the hospital with Mr. Ames and all home care therapists to bring him up to date on our work and to include him in planning for the time when Mrs. Ames would no longer need our specialized services and would be discharged from the home care program.

We had now done significant work in three of the four contracted areas—aide problems, Mrs. Ames' behavior, and Mr. Ames' emotional stresses. What remained was the problem of lack of family involvement. I felt that Mr. Ames was now strengthened to the point of being able to take control of this final aspect of our contract. I asked Mr. Ames and the aide to work with Mrs. Ames so she would not emit such frightening shrieks. I explained directly to Mrs. Ames that her daughter was upset by these shrieks, and that they were one reason why neither she nor the grandchildren visited. I further told her that I knew it was frustrating not to be able to be totally understood and that her shrieks were her way of "letting off steam," but it was not a helpful way, for it was keeping the people she loved away from her. I asked her, Mr. Ames, and the aide if they could think of better ways for Mrs. Ames to communicate her frustrations. Mr. Ames suggested she gently bang the table with her hand. Mrs. Ames agreed to try this method and was pleased that the idea came from her husband. Mr. Ames then said that he was having dinner with his daughter that night and he planned to tell her of today's session and how he and the aide were working with Mrs. Ames to help her communicate better.

I asked him if he felt his children and grandchildren might be helpful also. He said his wife would probably be less frightening to them now, but he did not know exactly what to ask of his family. I suggested that some of the many professional home care therapy visits might be eventually replaced by short family visits at regular intervals. His wife could put these scheduled visits on her calendar and look forward to having them. Mr. Ames agreed that a specific, limited involvement by their children and grandchildren would be a relatively easy request for him to make, and he would do so at dinner that night.

In this case, as in so much of my work, my focus was on strengthening both formal and informal support systems. Whether it is the hospital-based home care team, a professional home aide, family members, friends, or neighbors, I feel that the home care social worker's task is to perform skilled interventions, within a collaborative framework, to help those who have ongoing responsibility for patient care. My contact with patients is necessarily brief. At the beginning of a social work relationship, a family member such as Mr. Ames can become quite dependent, but the eventual goal is always to strengthen available home supports to function without professional assistance.

Chapter 3

The Eccentric Artist:
The Filial Role in Home Care
for the Frail Elderly

The late social worker Margaret Blenkner (1965) wrote:

> Social work must make possible, through rendering to old people in their homes, the services, the comfort, the affectional concern, and the dependability that is expected of and given by an adult child. . . . The professional worker need not be afraid to assume the filial role.

Miss Brady was seventy-one years old and had recently been diagnosed as being legally blind. Subject to hypertension, "little strokes," and blackouts, she suffered from memory loss and episodes of confusion. She fell often. Our hospital home care professional staff felt that it was unlikely she could continue to live alone at home. Miss Brady, however, hated to admit her increasing limitations and was determined to stay at home.

My work began the day after Miss Brady went home from the hospital. Calling to set up an appointment, I learned from the visiting nurse that the hospital staff had renewed cause for apprehension. Miss Brady had fallen that very morning and also had had one of her numerous blackouts during the nurse's visit. Fortunately, the home health aide, Ms. Field, was on hand twenty hours per week, and Miss Brady liked her.

That afternoon I climbed the stairs to Miss Brady's third-floor apartment and entered a high-ceilinged, artistically furnished living

---

This chapter originally appeared in *Practice Digest*, NASW, 3(2), September 1980, pp. 10-14.

room. It was dusty and faded with old plastic sheets on the furniture and lamps, but the general effect was orderly.

Miss Brady, perched cross-legged on a high wooden stool, was daintily eating eggs and toast in the kitchen area. She was wearing only a blue satin robe, which hung open and exposed a slender, surprisingly youthful body. She wore heels four inches high and seemed unaware of or unselfconscious about her appearance. Thus perched, she called out to me to sit on the plastic-covered sofa and wait for her in the living room.

The following three-way conversation took place. It gave me a sense of Miss Brady's colorful personality, her articulate speech, and also the fear beneath her self-confident exterior.

> **Miss B:** Sorry we can't talk now, but the nurse was here, I had to bathe, and I just now have time to eat.

> **LR:** That's okay, I'll wait. Sorry I interrupted your lunch.

> **Ms. F** (the home health aide): You know, she fell before the nurse came, blacked out today and yesterday, too. She can't stay alone.

> **Miss B:** What?

> **LR:** Ms. Field was telling me that you're blacking out, Miss Brady. How about sitting here so we can all hear one another?

> **Miss B:** Oh, blacking out. Yes, I've been doing that a while. I remember how impressed the Art Students League was when I told them I never remembered starting my paintings. I'd wake from a trance, the picture would be outlined before me, and then I'd fill in the details. You can look at my stuff while I eat.

> **LR:** It's beautiful work—and your other pieces are unusual, too.

> **Miss B:** Venetian glass, special china. I don't let anyone touch those exquisite things but me. [With an elegant, accurate flourish, she pulled the string that turned off a naked lightbulb. She

moved toward me shakily on those very high heels.] So, now I'm done. Why are you here?

LR: To see how things are going for you at home. I try to see most folks who leave the hospital on home care, because it can be upsetting to get used to home again. Three people at the hospital especially asked me to see you: Mrs. Frances, Mrs. Roth, and Miss Harper. [Miss Harper was the floor social worker.]

Miss B: Agh! I hated Miss Harper. What a small mind! You know, I've had such a full life, done things she's never heard of, had men who gave me anything I asked for. Of course I could never marry; I can't live with any man too long. I worked as a legal secretary. Too bad for me, it's all gone now. And now she has the nerve to tell me to go to a center with a bunch of old biddies! Have a new life learning Braille. I don't want to learn Braille! I don't like all you strange people coming into my home. I don't like all the phone calls. Why don't you leave me alone? [She clutched my arm.]

LR: I'm descending on you like all the rest, but I'm not sure you want me to leave.

Miss B: Well, pretty soon. I suddenly realized in the hospital that I'm over seventy. For the first time I thought, "That's old." Lucy, I don't feel old. Last year it started—the tingling in my arms, the falling; but if I fall, I fall.

LR: Sounds scary, though. What happens? Do you get a warning?

Miss B: Sometimes. Then I can sit. But if there's no time, I just go out for a minute or two, wake up on the floor, then get up and get on with my business. I can manage, but now that I can hardly see, it's better that Ms. Field is here. She's a good girl.

Ms. F: We hit it off right away.

LR: But she's here only twenty hours a week. Is that enough? How will you manage when she leaves tonight?

Miss B: Same as last night. I'll black out; I'll get up. Leave me alone. Leave.

Ms. F: She can't handle too much help around. I'll call in again tonight.

Miss B: I don't want to appear ungrateful.

LR: You want your privacy, and Ms. F is enough help for now.

Miss B: Call me next week.

As a result of that visit, I concluded that Miss Brady was sometimes accepting, sometimes in denial that she was sick and getting old; beyond that, she was terrified of dying. Although she valued her privacy and independence, she realized that the visiting nurse and health aide had practical value: their services kept her out of the hospital, which she hated.

My services were another story. She lumped me with Miss Harper, the floor social worker, who seemed to her to be patronizing and dryly professional. Miss Harper diagnosed and prescribed but seemed to be unaware of Miss Brady's eccentricities, strengths, and special needs.

On the other hand, I was on her own comfortable turf with time and interest to admire her achievements. Perhaps I would listen to her and stay around to keep her company. If not, well, she could make me leave, especially if I made her uncomfortable by bearing down on the reality of her situation.

The next day, Ms. Field did not show up. (She was ill and for some reason could not reach Miss Brady.) Miss Brady called me in a panic. I went over and also arranged for a replacement aide. This incident helped me gain her trust on a professional level.

Over the next two months, I made ten visits to Miss Brady, or Madeleine, as she asked me to call her. I also had numerous phone conversations about her with various community agencies. One of my contacts was Jackie, the local Medicaid caseworker, whom I grew to like as we talked on the phone. I described her affectionately to Madeleine, and on my recommendation, Jackie paid a visit. That helped us to start planning for replacement aide service after the hospital home care ended and Madeleine became eligible for Medicaid.

I also became a link to Madeleine's "informal network": counter girls at the local coffee shop, widowed patrons of the shop, fellow tenants, delivery men from the local stores. Alerted to Madeleine's poorer health, this informal support system stepped in to help as they could. Tenants did errands for her. The delivery men drove her to the doctor or on special errands. In addition, these helpers stayed and talked with Madeleine a long time. I could understand why. As a sort of compensation for her loss of health and eyesight, Madeleine reminisced about her past, her glorious career, and her social life. Her stories may have been exaggerations, but they were certainly entertaining.

Madeleine reminded me of a character, an unemployed actor, in Isaac Bashevis Singer's story "A Friend of Kafka." The actor's stories so delighted his listeners that they gladly paid him a "zloty" for every exotic tale. Surely Madeleine offered a similar incentive. Her caregivers had the chance to experience her charisma, her eccentricity, her sexuality.

I, too, shared in this reciprocity. I looked forward to her company and felt similarly rewarded. It was much like visiting an interesting friend or, as time went on, a fascinating aunt. By listening to her stories, admiring her achievements, putting up with her eccentricities, I was, in a sense, putting myself in the role she wanted me to play. But it was also, I believe, my assumption of a filial role that allowed Madeleine and me to make the progress we did. It allowed Madeleine, in the course of our two months together, to acknowledge her need of additional help from professional sources.

As Madeleine's condition improved, she would have her aide walk her to the coffee shop, where she talked with her friends while the aide shopped and did the laundry. That provided a social life, but Madeleine had begun to complain that she could not see well enough to write checks and attend to finances. She did not want her friends and neighbors to assume those chores.

When I spoke of the need to find a social agency to care for her (Medicare restrictions limited my own service), she abruptly stopped complaining. Instead, she laboriously began trying to read her own mail and write checks. She often spent whole days at these chores. I inferred that she was angry at me for talking about leaving and was trying to deny that she needed my help or anyone else's.

But trying to read and write on her own was frustrating. On my visits, we talked about Madeleine's losses—the loss of her eyesight, and soon the loss of me. The combination of her frustration and our talks led Madeleine to acknowledge that she did need help. I suggested The Lighthouse (a nonprofit organization for the blind) as a resource. It could teach her the skills she needed and also provide continued contact with a social worker. Madeleine agreed to try it.

Talking with a social worker at The Lighthouse, I described the filial approach I had used. The social worker there agreed to follow the same approach. We hoped that once Madeleine had acquired the skills she needed, the staff and clients of The Lighthouse might serve as an additional surrogate family.

I have come to see that social workers can take on a filial role far more easily in home health care than in hospitals or nursing homes. Because patients in those places have so few personal relationships, they seek to develop one with staff members. But their numbers are too large for this to occur. The collective, implicit demands of these patients can overwhelm a social worker and lead him or her to limit contact to formal and professional interactions.

Of course, even for a home care social worker, it is far easier to assume a filial role with a client such as Madeleine. A client who lacks her personality (another Singer character, Bessie Popkin, comes to mind) might have to rely on the neediness of her situation or the guilt others feel to inspire a similar kind of service.

Social workers themselves are not the only ones who can take on a filial role. Through their example they can help train a client's friends and neighbors to function as part-time caregivers. The social worker can present the idea of limits: being available for a limited period of time. (A neighbor who fears being continually on call might make a contract: "I can spend Sunday afternoons from 1 to 3 with you. I can't do anything more.") If that sounds overly calculated, we should recall that social workers themselves set limits on their contacts with clients. For example, we might say we are only available from 9 to 5; we are not on call at home; we create a contract, and we set termination dates. The ultimate benefit of this combination of personal and professional services is that it enables many clients frequently labeled "difficult" to stay in their homes.

REFERENCE

Margaret Blenkner. (1965). "Social Work and Family Relationships in Later Life with Some Thoughts on Filial Maturity," in Ethel Shanas and Gordon F. Streib (eds.), *Social Structure and the Family—Generational Relations.* Englewood Cliffs, NJ: Prentice-Hall, pp. 58-59.

Chapter 4

Elderly Home Care Clients: Maintaining Purpose in Life

Among the major factors determining happiness and optimism among the elderly are good health, adequate finances, a healthy spouse, and family and community supports, all of which contribute to maintaining self-esteem and a purpose in life.

Loss of health was the primary concern of the elderly whom I saw when I worked as a medical social worker within a hospital-based home care program. I intervened primarily in the home following hospital discharge, assessing problems and counseling patients and family members who were trying to cope with stresses directly related to a health crisis.

Great stress was associated with returning home without a leg, with a colostomy bag, or with a diagnosis of CVA or cancer. The home environment was often inadequate to meet the patient's needs. As the patient struggled to become more independent, he or she was hit full-force with various assaults to self-esteem—a damaged body image, loss of function, lowered social and economic status. The patient became depressed and often lost his or her sense of life's purpose.

Most of my elderly patients had had little contact with a social worker prior to their health crisis. They belonged to a generation that prided itself on its ability to deal with life's problems without turning to professionals for help; however, as caring family, friends, and hospital staff identified the elderly patient's distress as a nor-

This chapter was originally a presentation titled "Prevention and the Aging" at the Conference on Long-Term Care at the New York Academy of Medicine, June 19, 1980.

mal, very upsetting reaction to sudden medical illness or disability, long-held negative attitudes about counseling began to change. The stigma once attached to admitting emotional weakness decreased, because it was now firmly tied to a new physical problem.

Once a trusting casework relationship was established in the home, strong feelings of sorrow and frustration opened up, related not only to the present illness but to many other losses experienced before this illness—losses never fully grieved over, until now: loss of parents, siblings, children, friends; loss of jobs, money, status; loss of physical and mental functioning. Fears also surfaced about further deterioration; there were fears about dying.

The two home care cases described in this chapter illustrate the importance of "grief work" in maintaining health and a purpose in life. One concerns loss of a beloved person, the other loss of a creative outlet, exacerbating gastrointestinal illnesses in both cases.

Case number 1:

> Mrs. Meyers, age seventy-eight, was discharged from the hospital following a severe flare-up of ulcerative colitis. The visiting nurse reported she was also suffering from sleeplessness and depression. Her colitis symptoms began immediately after her husband's death, just one year ago. She had decided to immediately leave her long-time Brooklyn home and move to a new senior citizens housing complex in Manhattan. She had wanted to avoid any reminders of her husband. She had never mourned his death.

> I first helped Mrs. Meyers recognize the connection between the anniversary of her husband's death and her recent sleeplessness and depression, as well as her worsening colitis symptoms. For the first time, she discussed the agony of his final hours and poured out her feelings of loss and fear for the future. She spoke of other dead family members and how she missed her Brooklyn friends. She reminisced about their happy marriage, their loving companionship. She spoke of her continued need to be loved and have friends.

> As counseling progressed, Mrs. Meyers adjusted to some of her losses and was able to attend the senior center I had located near her building as part of my effort to increase her support-

ive network. She contributed furniture and books from her old home to the center. She made new friends, she slept better, and her depression lifted.

Depression can also be helped by a life review, with the goal of finding new or old interests and talents that can be modified to fit the elderly patient's present abilities. Sometimes these talents can be shared and taught to others.

Case number 2:

Mr. Simmons, age eighty, a bachelor with no family, had traveled the subway daily for forty years to his job in the garment district. The ride was long. He often became tired of reading his books and began to draw small, detailed pictures of his fellow passengers—some friends, some strangers—within the page margins. He had stopped drawing when he retired fifteen years ago. He was now at home with a diagnosis of colon cancer as well as a colostomy he could not manage well, which left him feeling ashamed, isolated, and depressed.

It was a hot August day when I made my first home visit, and it showed! Mr. Simmons commiserated about my long, hot subway ride by vaguely mentioning his old hobby. He listlessly showed me an old book with his drawings. I said that he seemed to me to be a talented caricaturist. Soon he was telling me fascinating stories of old subway experiences he had had involving these characters.

I then contacted a local community center where he told these illustrated character stories to various groups. He also taught an art class there. Sharing his talent through storytelling and teaching gave validity to Mr. Simmons' life. It gave him a greater sense of self-esteem, which in turn allowed him to tolerate the colostomy. Our grief work together was amazingly short.

Most of my patients lacked adequate financial resources. They had returned home from the hospital after an exacerbation of a long chronic illness and had become almost impoverished. Insurance covered professional nursing and social work home visits as well as limited home health aide services, but there was no reimbursement for the housekeeping services so essential to maintaining the elderly comfortably at home. Much of a chronically ill person's money was used to buy private, expensive housekeeping help.

I found financial resources for housekeeper payment by working with family members, community social service agencies, and Medicaid. My family interviews and persistent advocacy, despite bureaucratic mix-ups and delays, served as a role model and morale booster—not only for patients but for other family members, especially spouses. They saw hope that they need not shoulder the entire financial burden of home management.

This brings me to another factor determining happiness and optimism among the elderly—having a healthy spouse. Patients told me of their sense of guilt and of being a burden as they witnessed fatigue and tension developing in their mates. I began a caregiving group in a home care patient's apartment in order to strengthen spouses, so that they, too, could maintain a purpose in life (see Chapter 5). I invited four other home care spouses in the area, and they were all eager to join this group. We followed a self-help model, my role being one of facilitator. By the end of the first meeting, they changed the group into a couples' friendship group. They decided to bring their disabled or ill spouses to the next meeting (some in wheelchairs) and later rotate meetings in one another's homes. They had thought they would never be able to function socially as couples again. Now, meeting in one another's homes, their self-esteem was increased as they showed their new friends their household skills and talents and traded interests and resources.

Maintaining a purpose in life was often difficult for the infirm elderly I visited, considering the various threats to their self-esteem. Through the combined efforts of families, friends, and health care professionals from many disciplines, most elderly home health care patients survived their health crises, with its accompanying depression. They could and often did resume purposeful lives within their homes and communities.

Chapter 5

Caregivers and Their Ill Spouses: Creating a Health-Promoting Group for Elderly Couples in a Hospital Home Health Care Program

Geriatric social workers must often cope with the plight of an elderly couple—one of whom is ill, the other frail but still able to be a caregiver—who desperately want to remain together within their own community. These workers, doing case management in a variety of agency settings, can discover that their traditional casework home care plans are not adequate to help their clients avoid nursing home placement.

It is widely known that the Natural Supports Program of Community Service Society identified the caregivers' vital role in maintaining ill, elderly spouses at home and developed meaningful groups for them (Mellor, Rzetelny, and Audis, 1979). Videotapes have been produced for use in starting and maintaining support groups for caregivers of the impaired elderly (Zimmer, 1986).

What has not been done, however, is to give the patient, along with the caregiving spouse, peer group support in the home during an acute phase of illness. Social workers who make home visits as part of hospital-based home health care programs have a unique opportunity (following the crisis of hospitalization that so often leads to nursing home placement) to use their skills to create health-promoting groups for these needy couples. These health-promoting groups are capable of keeping impaired elderly couples together, actively involved at home, long after official home health care programs have ended.

The author wishes to thank Grace Fields, ACSW, for her help in preparing this chapter, which appeared in *Social Work in Health Care*, 11(4), Summer 1986, pp. 83-92.

The purpose of this chapter is to demonstrate how such a group can be created and to propose that certified home health care agencies incorporate such groups into their regular programs.

PRINCIPLES OF HEALTH-PROMOTING GROUP FORMATION

Healthy elderly married couples, like healthy people of any age, often move within informal networks or groups (family, friends, neighbors) and formal networks (social agencies, schools, religious organizations, banks). These social connections play an important supportive role in a couple's day-to-day living in their communities.

This supportive role becomes crucial when serious illness strikes a spouse, necessitating hospitalization and an anticipated state of extreme vulnerability when the spouse patient returns home. Yet in many instances, the community connections are inadequately equipped to integrate the patient back into his or her home environment. Portions of the network may hold, allowing the couple to plan for a return home but with considerable anxiety about their network's future availability and expertise. If the entire network breaks down, nursing home placement may become the only option.

In hospitals with certified home health care programs, elderly couples can obtain well-planned and coordinated services to augment and support the usual caring people in their lives. Registered nurses, nurses' aides, physical and occupational therapists, social workers and other professionals join the pre-illness network to ensure that the couples can return safely to their homes. Unfortunately, these excellent programs are short-term, the average length of stay being two to three months, and the couples' networks again become jeopardized, since most patients are not fully well when home care terminates.

A health-promoting group can infuse long-term informal supports into impaired elderly couples' home networks, giving them a better chance to stay at home. The formation of such a group requires the implementation of five principles:

1. The home care social worker becomes a filial professional by blending the theories of Dobrof and Litwak (1977) and Blenk-

ner (1965) and embodying them in his or her casework and groupwork practice (Rosengarten, 1980). These theories speak about "shared functions and balanced coordination between formal and informal systems" and about providing the elderly with a "good child." The social worker becomes not only the formal system's representative, with clear goals and access to various concrete resources, but also the informal system's family member, emotionally involved and able to meet idiosyncratic needs. The filial professional enters and strengthens both existing support systems and then moves on to create the health-promoting group—a network addition. This is a very flexible way of working and vastly increases the home care case manager's opportunities to help elderly couples remain at home.

2. The worker's interventions take place immediately after an acute period of illness and bring together the patient as well as the caregiver in a long-term group that meets regularly in each patient's own home.

3. The ongoing social work role is indispensable to the group because fluctuations in the physical and emotional condition of the couples prevent them from becoming a self-help group, and because the couples value the social worker's affiliation with their hospital.

4. The new group formed assures that no single agency or person in the couples' network ever receives too much responsibility for caregiving duties, thereby lessening the chance of nursing home placement.

5. The security and peace of mind provided by group formation increases the self-esteem, self-confidence, and creativity of elderly couples, enabling them in turn to positively affect and energize other group members. Thus, the elderly have the gratifying opportunity of feeding back into the group, as well as receiving benefits from its operation.

FORMING THE GROUP

The following pages will describe the process by which the filial professional social worker recruited four couples from her home care caseload, and then used group work techniques to help them become the Caregivers and Spouses Group. The couples chosen, the Adamses, Browns, Collinses, and Donners (names created to help the reader identify them more easily) all lived near one another on the Upper West Side of Manhattan, across Central Park from their hospital, Mt. Sinai.

The Adamses

When Albert Adams, age seventy, came into the hospital for cardiac arrhythmia, he and his wife had had five years of successful retirement, after forty years of a good marriage and joint operation of a small grocery store.

They had attended the local community center for discussion groups, bridge, and day trips. They had traveled, spending time with friends and visiting their engineer son in California. After a month's physical confinement, however, Albert was unable to walk safely without assistance. Both he and his wife had residual unsteady gaits from childhood polio. The combination of Albert's other chronic problems, parkinsonism and poor vision, along with his heart problems, necessitated home care services: a visiting nurse to monitor his heart medications, a physical therapist to remobilize his walking, and a twenty-hour weekly home health aide to help him with his walking and personal care needs. Albert and Alice felt supported by their new helpers. Alice was grateful for freedom from many household functions, and felt free to attend center activities and visit friends, knowing Albert was well cared for even though his vision had worsened and his ability to walk alone did not return.

No sooner were they accustomed to this arrangement than it was time for it to be discontinued. Medicare maximum for this chronic level of care had been reached. The visiting nurse saw that Alice was panicking. Albert was depressed. The social worker was called in.

Traditional casework might have helped this couple to grieve their losses, to accept limitations and dependency, and then to spend down their savings to reach Medicaid eligibility for home attendant services. A review of the couple's use of social group networks in the past and their positive response to the medical network of services recently provided suggested to the social worker that the Adamses were good health-promoting group prospects. The social worker began by speaking of her own family, of her personal knowledge of and respect for the Adamses' physician, and of her love of music. Albert, sensing an ally, passionately described how carefully he used Alice's absences from the house while the aide was there. He would turn the stereo up and enjoy his favorite records, often singing the melodies. Alice tensely replied that she could not tolerate such "noise" around her. It was bad enough being cooped up in the house, hard enough managing the wheelchair on their occasional outings, without also enduring Bartók blasting through their home. The worker sympathized, citing her own dislike of the rock music that sometimes assailed her ears when her own adolescents opened their bedroom door. The worker then suggested that Albert call a nearby music school, offering a room to a classical music student in exchange for twenty hours of aide-type service. This step would enlarge the Adamses' network, giving them, through bartering, an informal aide through the formal system (school) and possibly another "son," thereby returning their network to its previously high level of functioning.

The plan worked. The music student first wheeled Albert to the eye doctor and got him a prescription, then new glasses, which somewhat improved Albert's reading ability. Albert now had another activity to do quietly whenever he was alone with Alice. The student brought new music to Albert, enlarging his musical repertoire. They both loudly sang along with their favorite Verdi arias, and Albert even learned a few modest conducting techniques. Alice returned to the center.

Albert's walking, however, never really improved, and Alice sadly learned from her physician that she had beginning signs of arthritis. The Adamses felt their problems were increasing; they began to explore future long-term care needs with the social worker beyond twenty hours of aide help. The worker informed them that she was presently seeing three other elderly couples who lived near the Adamses on her home care caseload and who were all coping with medical illnesses following hospital discharge. Indeed, the worker had obtained her idea of employing the music student as an aide from one of these couples. Might not these elderly patients learn to handle certain issues better by talking to one another in their own homes as a group?

The Adamses loved the idea. It was a new community project, somewhat like their previous experiences and well suited to their personalities. It might become an ideal resocialization and resource-sharing group. Who could better understand their present problems than other home care patients? The Adamses immediately asked the worker to invite another home care couple in the area to their home to plan for the first Caregivers and Spouses Group meeting. The social worker thought of the Browns.

The Browns

The Browns were a couple whose forty-year marriage (both were sixty-five) had always been competitive. Betty, the patient, had had a colostomy and was now suffering from advanced arthritis. She never left her home. She was physically frail but emotionally powerful because of her family's status, money, and her strong intellect. Her attorney husband, Barry, was both intellectually and physically fit but financially insecure. They had managed as long as each of them maintained a strong separate network of friends and professional associates. Now a marital problem with their daughter and son-in-law had given Barry new, improved weapons with which to attack Betty. Betty responded by bleeding into her colostomy, requiring hospitalization and later involvement in the home care program.

In the course of the social worker's sessions with them, the Browns made constructive compromises. Barry agreed to help his daughter obtain a quiet divorce, while Betty agreed to finance a long-desired business venture of Barry's. They were then ready for the first time in years to try socializing together, and the worker suggested the Caregivers and Spouses Group. Barry eagerly came to the Adamses for the planning session for the initial group meeting and asked if the next meeting could be held at his home, where they could meet Betty. They also wanted the social worker to invite another couple.

The Collinses

The Collinses, both in their seventies, needed a group. The question was how to connect them. Their past frightening experiences did not predispose them to dependency even on professional help, let alone sharing with strangers. They were survivors who had escaped oppression under Hitler then expropriation under Castro. They had come to New York, set up a small dress shop, learned a third language and culture, and educated a daughter, now a teacher. When Carol Collins went on home care after hospitalization for an exacerbation of her arthritis, she and her husband had difficulty accepting an aide, preferring help from their already burdened daughter. However, for Carol there had been, through social work home visits, movement toward trusting professionals, helping her direct herself toward the outside world. She was able to hire the aide privately after home care terminated so that she could have help with shopping and getting out to visit the community center.

Carl, on the other hand, retired for ten years and lacking nonwork interests, reported to the social worker that he was more discontented as he stayed home alone, still unwilling to mix "with the old folks" and missing his wife when she went to the senior center.

Readiness for the group came by crisis. A healthier Carol, with her arthritis in remission, could no longer bear remaining at home with her complaining husband. She packed a bag and left home. Carl came running into the social worker's hospital office, begging the worker to convince his wife to return home. The worker located Carol at a nearby hotel and found her confused and without funds. Medication and psychiatric intervention appeared to be needed. Carol was no longer officially on the hospital's home care program, so a community social agency was enlisted. Their psychiatrist immediately responded, prescribed medication, and scheduled marital counseling sessions.

Now both the Collinses realized they needed more in their lives. The worker recommended the newly forming Caretakers and Spouses Group, particularly Betty Brown, the homebound arthritic invalid. Carol was fascinated by the personality difference between herself and Betty, as described by her worker. Carl conceded that the described men might be "worth his time."

The Collinses thus joined the Adamses at the Browns' home for the first Caregivers and Spouses Group meeting.

The group expressed joy that they were resocializing as couples for the first time in years with people who really understood their special problems. Betty was impressed by Carol's vitality and persistence in fighting her arthritis. Carl and Albert were impressed by Barry's business acumen, and all traded animated tales of the past and present. Carol told the group how she loved opera. Betty stated that she never missed a televised opera. Albert, thrilled with their interest, offered to lend Betty his student to push her wheelchair, and they could all attend an opera together. Betty slowly and darkly declined, hinting at her deep, long-standing emotional problems that prevented her from leaving her home. This mysterious disclosure greatly intrigued all the group members, except her husband, Barry. Alice and Carol supportively promised to call Betty between meetings, establishing a telephone network.

Betty was being recognized as a witty, fascinating spinner of tales, and her self-esteem and desire to communicate grew as she warmed to the group's appreciation of her talents. The group was now firmly launched, as the social worker considered adding the Donners.

The Donners

When the social worker first visited the Donners, their isolation was evident. They had no friends in the building or in the community where they had lived for forty years. David Donner, seventy-five, a retired barber, had parkinsonism. After he suffered a fractured hip from a fall at home, his wife, Dolly, sixty-five, spent her days caring for him. All he needed, he said, was Dolly—her talents, love, and buoyancy. Dolly, an expressive, dramatic woman, had played the piano professionally but at David's insistence had given up her career after marriage. Following his hospitalization, David's demands became excessive, and Dolly's fatigue, anxiety, and anger built until she refused to continue their nightly routine of playing David's favorite songs. Both became depressed. When the worker spoke about the group meeting, David encouraged Dolly to join the worker at the meeting to help her "return to her old self" but declined to go himself, preferring to watch television and read.

Dolly came to the meeting but was nervous and agitated, called her husband three times, dwelled on the details of his illness, and finally rushed home before the meeting's end. The group told the worker Dolly was too theatrical, nervous, and dominating; they thought she would not "fit in." Dolly had sensed the group's rejection, which reinforced her need to continue to isolate herself.

FITTING IN

During several subsequent casework home visit interviews with the social worker, David Donner examined his demanding behavior related to his fears about continued physical losses and death, and Dolly unleashed her long, smoldering resentment against David about her lost musical career. Dolly agreed to play for him again. The worker, in an effort to further grasp the needs and strengths of this couple, shifted to the filial role. She listened to their music and joined in piano duets. Dolly suddenly became a poised authoritative teacher, calmly correcting the worker's shaky technique. The worker and David were both impressed by Dolly's teaching skills. All traces of her characteristic anxiety vanished while she was teaching. David suggested Dolly teach a couple of students at home. The worker wondered if Dolly would play a concert in her home for the Caretakers and Spouses Group. Both ideas appealed to Dolly.

The worker told the group about Dolly's musical abilities. They could now accept Dolly Donner redefined as artist and teacher. Alice Adams prepared and sent out invitations. Betty Brown and Carol Collins called Dolly frequently to arrange concert details. Dolly placed an ad for students on her lobby's bulletin board, and two children began piano lessons and came to the concert. David met Carl Collins at Dolly's concert and found him especially understanding. They became friends, and the Donners were welcomed into the group.

LATER ACTIVITIES

Group meetings rotated among all members' homes, giving each couple opportunities not only to be host and hostess for the first time in years but to display various aspects of their personalities, represented by their own individual home environments.

A city-sponsored radio station asked the worker to speak about the group. The worker brought Alice and Albert to the station by cab, and for forty-five minutes, the three discussed the founding, development, and present meaning of the Caretakers and Spouses Group, various urban and health problems of the handicapped elderly, and Medicare limitations. It was an exciting experience for all; the Adamses felt, and indeed were, very important. The radio station manager presented Alice with a tape of the program, which Alice played at the next group meeting, then took over to play for Betty, who had missed both program and meeting. Alice also mailed a copy of the tape to her son, who expressed pride in his parents' activities.

The group planned a trip to the aquarium, home lectures from other hospital personnel, and visits with local politicians to listen to their concerns and teach them lobbying techniques. Along with social activities they wanted to work for better home health care benefits. They agreed to rotate through one another's homes, sharing resources and talents, and exchanging recipes, reminiscences, and resources they had found. Telephone assurance would continue. In short, they planned to continue to provide one another an expanding, enriching network through a health-promoting group.

UNFINISHED BUSINESS

As the group developed its own life and leadership, Alice Adams emerged as the indigenous leader. They considered becoming totally a self-help group without the social worker. Alice spoke for the group. Often she and other members could take leadership roles, when they felt physically and emotionally healthy; however, it was the nature of their chronic illnesses that they had both good and bad days. They decided that they needed ongoing professional social work leadership to keep their health-promoting network strong.

IMPLICATIONS AND OBSERVATIONS

In geriatric home care, using supportive groups, the social worker has a unique opportunity to provide humane, professional, psychosocial assessments and, hopefully, to restore and improve the home health network group of the elderly to optimum physical, mental, and social functioning. By strengthening these mutual aid-givers to operate comfortably within the home environment, the social worker creates an economically and humanistically sound solution to the long-term care needs of the sick elderly and encourages participation by all members of the group. Even the loss of a primary caregiver, through illness or death, will not destroy this strong, enriched group network—nor will the loss of services provided by Medicare home care once the acute phase of the illness has passed.

This experience took place in a professional hospital home care and social work climate where creativity and innovation were encouraged. A home care caseload is basically "short-term." Funding through Medicare ceases after two to three months when the case is judged to no longer require "skilled nursing care," and aid is terminated. This effort, however, extended beyond that time, due to the Social Work Services Department's approval. However, the group's continuation was not mandated administratively during absences or change of workers, and, therefore, it did not continue after the worker left the agency.

At present group work is not a standard part of hospital home health care. Group work with elderly couples in hospital-based home health care can happen as a result of worker enthusiasm and vision. It may be tolerated or even blessed by "the department," but it is not required or expected. The kind of effort described in this chapter is operable and needed in many hospital home care programs. How can this come about? Good record keeping and the strong involvement of a supervisor or administrator in the effort are among the ways that workers can assure that group work will be viewed as part of the worker's "real," rather than idiosyncratic, assignment. It is easier for a worker to establish the validity of a piece of a program than to institutionalize it, but both are critical if the program is to survive.

Can funding be redirected so that such efforts are part of the formal, funded arrangement in regular home care programs? Should such support be hospital-based? Could the effort be initiated by the hospital and transferred to a community-based agency? Could a private practice worker offer this service at an affordable fee for the group? Would this meet the group's need for feeling that they must have someone attached to their hospital who understood that their strength and capacity to function are uneven? Could that fear have been dissipated in time, or was it a valid intuition that, once cut loose from professional hospital help, finding the right door for help would be a difficult search?

The elderly population is growing. Hospital home care social workers and others involved with the growing number of geriatric patients are able to project from their work loads the risks and the strengths represented by this population. Out of such findings can come our capabilities to move planning and funding systems toward recognizing the importance of developing reliable health-promoting groups. The final purpose of this chapter, then, is to challenge social workers in hospital home care to participate in such brave planning.

REFERENCES

Blenkner, M. (1965). "Social Work and Family Relationships in Later Life, with Some Thoughts on Filial Maturity." In E. Shanas and G. F. Streib, *Social Structure and the Family: Generational Relations*, Englewood Cliffs, NJ: Prentice-Hall, pp. 58-59.

Dobrof, R. and E. Litwak. (1977). "Maintenance of Family Ties of Long Term Care Patients: Theory and Guide to Practice." Washington, DC: Department of Health, Education, and Welfare, pp. 86-87.

Mellor, M. J., H. Rzetelny, and I.E. Audis. (1979). "Self-Help Groups for Caregivers of the Aged: Natural Supports Program of Community Service Society of New York." Paper presented at First Annual Symposium, Social Work with Groups. Cleveland, December 1.

Rosengarten, L. (1980). "Taking on a Filial Role to Care for Frail Elderly." *Practice Digest*, September, pp. 10-14.

Zimmer, A. H. (1986). "Video Projects." *The Brookdale Center on Aging Newsletter*, Hunter College/CUNY, January, 8(2), p. 9.

PART II: COOPERATIVE HOME CARE IN COMMUNITY-BASED AGENCIES

As we have seen in Chapter 5, in my last year of work at Mount Sinai Hospital agency constraints prevented me from integrating the health-promoting group into the normal work routine of a traditional certified home care agency. But, as indicated in the Introduction, it was precisely at this time, in the summer of 1981, that I had the opportunity to travel with my husband—a professor of Italian who was about to begin an assignment as Study Abroad Director—to learn about cooperativism in geriatric home care in Bologna, Italy. This collaboration with my husband explains in good part the use of a more academic approach to the subject matter in Chapter 6. Chapter 7 has a didactic form, due to my attempt to translate the findings of Chapter 6 into terms useful for training home health aides.

The two chapters contain many examples of the theoretical and practical underpinnings of cooperative home care, first at the agency CADIAI in Bologna, then at COHME in New York City, during the first difficult years of its history. Operating within the format of an in-service for COHME's aides, I struggled to fulfill the traditional instructional needs of our New York State licensed home care agency while giving our workers content that reflected my Bologna experience. I always had to keep in mind the differences between the political cultures of Bologna and New York City. But I also had the advantage of working with women, many of whom came from societies where principles of cooperativism were readily accepted, often as a group norm; moreover, their religious training and beliefs provide a natural support for cooperativism.

Chapter 6

Aspects of Cooperative Home Care
for the Elderly in Bologna, Italy

From August 1981 to July 1982, my husband and I spent most of our time in Italy working in our respective areas of interest: he as director of a university consortium Study Abroad program and I interviewing people involved in the organization of health and social services for the elderly in Bologna. With the help of my husband as an interpreter whenever possible, I conducted numerous interviews with social workers, aides, nurses, physicians, administrators, elected and appointed political leaders, union officials, and, most important, with the workers and administrative personnel of a privately managed cooperative home care agency, CADIAI, standing for Cooperativa Assistenza Domiciliare Infanzia, Anziani, Infermi, that is, Cooperative Home Care for Children, the Elderly, and the Chronically Ill.

For my husband, much of whose scholarly work over the previous twenty-five years had been concerned with the cultural politics of the Italian Left, there was no better place to learn more about this subject firsthand than Bologna, the capital city of the region of Emilia-Romagna in Italy's "Red Belt." In this region, since the end of World War II, approximately 50 percent of the population had consistently voted for city administrations governed either by the Italian Communist Party or by coalitions of Communists and Socialists.

As far as I was concerned, Bologna provided opportunities to verify the extent to which the city's reputation for progressive social

---

A different version of this chapter appeared in *The PRIDE Institute Journal of Long Term Home Health Care*, 9(3), Summer 1990, pp. 33-37.

policy had affected the organization of services for the frail elderly. One of my main concerns was the low status and poor working conditions of geriatric aides in New York City. I wanted to find out whether the general principles of cooperativism and socialism, even if constrained as in Bologna by a capitalistic economy, had really been translated into the practices of daily life as they applied to the situation of the elderly.

I began a research project that at first centered on a comparison between New York City and Bologna with regard to the hospital experience, system of discharge planning, and posthospital care for elderly orthopedic patients. I soon realized, however, that as interesting and important as the orthopedic focus of my study was, there were other more original facets of care for the elderly in Bologna which merited a greater claim on my attention. Chief among these were the training and high quality of home care aides, especially those who worked in concert with the city aides as members of CADIAI. Other features of the Bolognese health system that attracted my attention were the city's senior citizen centers; the Pensioners Union; the political and communicative skills of community-based social workers and of organizers of cooperatives in the social service sector; and the emphasis in Bologna on grassroots, decentralized decision making.

CADIAI

I first heard about CADIAI from Anna Lopes-Pegna, the Director of Health Services in the Department of Social Security for the region of Emilia-Romagna. She was a widely known theorist of *protagonismo* in the workplace, which means helping people to become the main characters in the dramas of their lives. She told me that this cooperative agency had succeeded in upgrading the dignity of home care workers through programs of systematic education, group problem-solving techniques, close supervision, and in-service training conducted in a nonauthoritarian, democratic fashion.

I was referred for additional information to Sonia Scavo, a professional organizer for the League of Cooperatives belonging to the Italian General Confederation of Labor (CGIL). She had recently been assigned to CADIAI as a vice president. The CGIL, one of

Italy's three national labor federations, was founded in 1906. It is a vast conglomeration of millions of industrial, agricultural, professional, and service workers, including those employed by the country's large cooperative sector. Unlike the United States, where most trade unions are affiliated with the Democratic Party, in Italy the Socialist and Communist Parties claim the loyalty of many workers. The CGIL, like the two other labor federations associated with the Catholic and Social Democratic movements, trains people to give direction to newly created cooperative enterprises.

I learned that CADIAI was founded in 1974 by a group of mainly middle-class Bolognese women who had become aware of limitations on the home care services provided by the city, and of the plight of many poor women who were working as aides off the books for meager wages, without benefits, without agency connections, and without security. The founders of CADIAI, Scavo explained, aimed to give home care workers the full dignity to which they were entitled by applying the principle of group self-management. They saw this principle as the core of cooperativism, which could prevent the usual schism between workers and administrators. They wished to replace what was considered a haphazard, exploitative, and unproductive system with one that functioned in the best interests of both clients and workers. A crucial element of this cooperative core was an interdisciplinary team effort. Unlike the United States, where such a team is often composed of physician, nurse, and social worker, the CADIAI concept was based on the idea of collaboration among social workers, aides, nurses, and administrative staff, all sharing in decision making and in the organization of daily work practice according to their abilities and experience.

CADIAI saw itself as a third force in the field of home care for the elderly, the other two being the network of city aides and the local Catholic Church parishes, which for centuries had rendered assistance, formally and informally, to the families of the sick, the elderly, and the needy.

In 1979, after several years of experience with private clients from the more affluent sectors of Bolognese society who could afford its services, CADIAI entered into a contractual agreement with the city government to provide care for needy elderly. The

agreement stipulated that CADIAI-trained aides would work together with city aides in some of Bologna's eighteen administrative
areas, called *quartieri*, each of which is subdivided into districts
serving an elderly population of six to seven thousand. (Approximately 20 percent of Bologna's 475,000 inhabitants are over the age
of sixty.)

Before considering the relationship between CADIAI and the
city aides, it is important to take note of the way in which CADIAI
meetings were run.

I attended four two- to three-hour meetings for the group of aides
who specialized in the care of the elderly; they numbered about half
of the agency's seventy-two active workers. At one meeting, the
following issues were openly and often angrily raised by the aides:
wages, holiday schedules, the quality of in-service courses, whether
to continue the series of lectures to CADIAI aides by gynecologists,
how to deal with the special psychological and physical needs of the
elderly, how to help the elderly clients become resocialized after
illness, determining priorities within severe time constraints, and
how to report poor medical care. Perhaps too much was covered in
these sessions, but I felt that this chance to be listened to attentively
by a caring managerial staff, including social workers, enhanced the
aides' sense of personal worth and afforded the opportunity to
ventilate frustrations that can build up in anyone who performs
daily hands-on care for the sick elderly.

At another meeting, I learned that the aides hired by CADIAI
were somewhat better educated than their counterparts in the city-
run system and that their status as worker/partners was believed to
contribute to their high level of commitment to their jobs. Worker/
partners had their pay and bonuses directly deposited into an
agency-owned bank account and carried passbooks, which they
updated regularly. The contractual agreement between CADIAI and
the city government required that when CADIAI aides were hired
by the city they were to work a minimum of thirty-six hours a week
at the same average salary earned by the city aides, $4.00 an hour.
(The equivalent of $4.00 in lire in 1982 had the purchasing power
of about $5.50 in a comparable urban center in the United States.)
When CADIAI aides worked for private clients, their wages were
slightly less than those paid by the city.

Regarding the relationship between CADIAI and the city-run system of home care for the elderly, I observed tensions due to differences in social and educational backgrounds and also due to the frustrations encountered daily by the city aides who, in addition to handling enormous caseloads, had to contend with tedious bureaucratic procedures and a lack of the type of supportive structure provided by an agency such as CADIAI. Whereas most of the CADIAI aides lived in town, the city aides usually came from the provinces and had to cope with long train or bus rides to and from their homes every day. The city aides felt that CADIAI pampered its workers, and this attitude provoked some outbursts of resentment and perhaps jealousy. In almost all instances, however, the city social workers who were effectively in charge of the polyclinics located in the various districts (the doctors officially in charge were usually out on cases or for other reasons were not easily available) managed to maintain relatively cordial relations between their overworked colleagues and the CADIAI aides.

During the year I spent in Bologna, the committee of the Bologna City Council that oversees home care was headed by Antonio Belcastro, a member of the Italian Socialist Party, who told us of the city administration's hope to enhance the *protagonismo* of the elderly. This simply meant that the elderly themselves should assume as much responsibility as possible for their life choices in order to overcome "a passive, welfare mentality." This emphasis on helping the elderly become the active protagonists of their own lives was central to the philosophy of CADIAI as well, as we had previously learned from Anna Lopes-Pegna. To fulfill the promise of *protagonismo*, home care aides must have psychological and social understanding in addition to technical skills. It was our feeling that the in-service courses offered by CADIAI and the agency's philosophy of cooperative self-management engendered such understanding. Indeed, a part of the agency's mission, as stated in its founding charter, was "to offer, through its partner-aides, home care to the elderly for the purpose of guaranteeing their care and stimulating their autonomy and socialization."

The CADIAI in-service courses were conceived as central to the professionalization of home care work. In addition to the traditional topics covered in home health aide training programs in the United

States, CADIAI's required courses for its aides (which were attended voluntarily) included lectures given by outside experts from the fields of politics, law, and public administration. The aides also made regular visits to community social service agencies to learn about their activities and resources.

In addition to its rootedness in Italian political and social history, CADIAI's work should also be seen in relation to two contemporary features of Bolognese sociopolitical life: the activities of the senior centers and the work of the Pensioners Union, the *Sindacato Pensionati Italiani* affiliated with the General Confederation of Labor.

Senior centers are located in all of Bologna's eighteen districts. These centers are run by volunteers, and they are financed in part by tax levy funds and in part by the elderly members themselves. The head of the Bologna City Council committee overseeing home care played a leading role in establishing these centers. The real pioneer in establishing the senior centers in Bologna, however, was Rosa Marchi, a member of the Pensioners Union who, in 1976, saved a house destined for destruction and converted it into a thriving senior center in the Barca district of the city.

In this area of work, New York City, with its long history of settlement houses and neighborhood community centers, has much to teach the rest of the world. What Bologna has contributed with specific regard to senior centers is its program of planned interaction between their members and the various segments of the population who would not ordinarily come into contact with retired and elderly people. For some years now, the centers have arranged visits of the elderly to schools, factories, farms, hospitals, and other institutions, where they talk in an informal manner about their work and general life experiences. This effort has gone a long way to overcoming the sense of alienation suffered by so many of the elderly.

The Pensioners Union is led by highly politicized retired workers. The head of the Pensioners Union in Bologna, Gherardo Ghini, and his colleagues thought of social services as rights due to citizens who have contributed to the community during their work lives and who wish to continue to contribute as actively as possible after their retirement. He further believed that adequate incomes and medical insurance must be available to retired persons in order for them to remain active and involved citizens. The Pensioners Union struggles to protect the rights of the elderly retired workers of Italy in precisely these areas. As far as home care assistance for the elderly was concerned, Pensioners Union activists were aware of the need for all kinds of help and extended it whenever possible, especially as handymen, tour leaders, and occasional organizers of special transportation for elderly people who needed to be conveyed from their homes to physical rehabilitation centers.

As we ended our year in Bologna in the summer of 1982, it seemed to me and to my husband that what we had learned in our Italian experience could become a novel and exciting feature of social work home care practice in New York City. At that time, of course, I was only partially aware of the problems I would face in translating this experience into terms that were realistic in a very different setting. The subject of the next chapter—cooperative in-service training for home care aides—turned out to be one of the more easily translatable aspects of my work from the mid-1980s to the present.

Chapter 7

COHME's First In-Service on Cooperativism

The following in-service lecture and exchange of ideas between myself and a group of COHME aides took place on March 21, 1991, as part of the agency's sixth anniversary celebration. The in-service also served as a review and critique of COHME's cooperative development over the preceding five years. The relative lack of interventions by the aides should not be interpreted as their lack of interest in the subject. It was due instead to my belief that, in order to present in-service material in a manner acceptable to the Department of Health, which licensed us, a lecture format with only occasional responses by the aides was preferable to an open discussion.

Lucy: Don't we often say things like: "Gee, she really cooperates with me; she's lots of fun to work with!" or "I feel just like part of a family working here!" or even "Well, she does her work OK, but she upsets me—she just doesn't cooperate." We sort of instinctively know a cooperative situation when we see it, don't we? We can feel it in the atmosphere of an office, a coffee shop, a restaurant the moment we enter it. What do you instinctively think of when you work cooperatively or when you see and feel you're in a cooperative atmosphere?

Replies: Unity, togetherness, sharing, helping each other.

Lucy: Those are good answers. Writers in the field of cooperativism have used similar statements, such as: "There are fewer tensions. I feel I have a stake in the organization. People are happy and productive in their work. There's a good feeling toward coworkers. There's a sense of being listened to. You feel cared about" (Kohn, 1986).

One definition of a cooperative home care agency is that it's nonprofit. Sometimes it's easier to understand "nonprofit" if we think of its opposite, which is _____?

Replies: Profit, money making.

Lucy: Right! Profit, or for-profit home care companies need to make money for their owners and shareholders. How they do this is a complicated process beyond the scope of our discussion tonight, but it does seem to me that many people who work for profit-based home care agencies have to concentrate a lot of their energy on making enough money to return to their investors. A nonprofit home care agency such as COHME is set up as a charity and is helped by grants and loans from foundations, government sources, concerned individuals, and/or agency board member donations. Grants, gifts, and donations do not have to be returned, but, of course, donors usually ask for reports on how their money was spent. Those who give money to COHME give because they believe in our *mission*, and want to support us. Naturally, loans to COHME have to be paid back.

I just mentioned our mission. Like charity, mission is another distinctive feature of nonprofit agencies. Mission is what we believe in, why we exist. Our mission, which you see prominently displayed in the COHME office, says:

WHY COHME EXISTS:
TO PROVIDE EXCELLENT HOME CARE TO FRAIL
    AND SICK ELDERLY
TO PROVIDE EXCELLENT JOBS FOR OUR WORKERS

We truly believe in our mission. We are in business to accomplish our mission, not to make large profits. We can accumulate money, but it's not "profit" it's called "cash reserve," and this cash reserve money never goes to benefit any outside person, but is always used to further the mission of COHME. We are currently trying to increase our cash reserve to enable us to offer health insurance and pension benefits to all our workers, as part of "providing excellent jobs for our workers."

Another difference between our nonprofit agency and for-profit agencies is that we address *need*, not *want*. This means that when an elderly person or his or her family calls COHME *wanting* a housekeeper at any cost to keep the apartment neat because the elderly person is tired of doing it herself or himself, we would refer that person to another agency. The client is not ill and has no medical needs. It's not an appropriate job for you with your home health aide skills; there is no diagnosed medical indication for our care, and we *need* a doctor's involvement to begin our services.

Nonprofits like COHME have *boards*. We have a board composed of community and professional leaders, whose expertise and advice we rely on a great deal to guide us.

We like solving community health problems of the elderly; we are idealistic; we are trusting; we hope to make a difference in the quality of life of our sick elderly clients and their families; and we like being true to our mission. That's all part of being a nonprofit home care agency (Carpenter, 1990)—our first defined characteristic of COHME's cooperative.

Let us try to get closer to what else cooperativism is or what we want it to be at COHME. Since opposites seemed helpful before, let us think about what is the opposite of cooperativism. Any ideas?

Replies: Being noncooperative, stubborn, selfish, discord, self-satisfied, putting yourself before others.

Lucy: Those are excellent ideas, and I'll be speaking directly about those very ideas a bit later. Now, let me tell you how some researchers look at the opposite of cooperativism—competition.

In its worst form, competition means gaining success by making others fail! That is rather upsetting to think about, isn't it? Competition can be devastating to many people and can contribute to feelings of anxiety, selfishness (your word), self-doubt, low self-esteem, and poor communication.

Our country, wonderful as it is in so many ways, is acknowledged to be the most competitive society in the world. Look how we organize our work, schools, games, and other leisure activities. Competition is deeply ingrained into our culture. It's part of our daily lives. We just do not usually stop and look hard at it, as we have the opportunity to do tonight. Let's look at Little League, the children's baseball organization we may remember playing in or watching when we were kids, or that our kids, grandchildren, or neighbors watch or participate in today.

A very upset writer has characterized Little League as "frantic, frothing parents humiliating their children in their quest for vicarious triumph" (Kohn, 1986, p. 92), or, I guess, putting the thought into longer, but simpler language: parents being wildly competitive by putting their kids through a game that makes the kids feel bad, instead of the parents openly competing themselves.

This is a very strong view, and we all know parents and kids who don't behave this way over a sport. Still, studies have shown that over 80 percent of kids who start participating in sports drop out by age fifteen, because they feel they are just "not good enough." Why should a kid have to stop playing a game he or she loves because he or she cannot win enough times? Even some kids who do win a lot stop playing sports because of the intense anxiety they experience as they have to fight off new competition, or worry about the next boy or girl who's "coming up," and will arrive any day to beat them.

So, there's no security for athletes, even in winning. Why can't we just play games to have a good time? We are socialized to think games have to be competitive. Kids in the U.S. say: "How can this be a game, if no one wins?" yet studies have shown that kids really prefer noncompetitive games, once they are exposed to them.

Here's an example of competitivness in school. Suzy waves her hand frantically in class: "I know! I know the answer!" She attracts the teacher's attention, is recognized by the teacher, and then Suzy suddenly looks confused. She says: "Uh, what was the question again?" Suzy was so eager to beat out her classmates that she lost track of the topic of discussion.

When Suzy, or any of us, focus on ourselves too much, putting ourselves forward too much (again, one of your definitions of competition), we can easily lose track of the issues involved. We can become so preoccupied with just winning that we get distracted from the task at hand. Suzy, as a grown woman, might become a highly competitive person who hides information, and alienates, frightens, or threatens other people who really could assist and support her in her work activities. For example, by not discussing her tasks with her co-workers, she has to independently spend her time and skills on problems that might have been already encountered, worked on, and/or solved by others.

Do you remember any incidents of competition hurting you or someone you care about—in a game, at school, at work, or somewhere else?

Aide: I'm pushing my son into Stuyvesant high school, and I shouldn't be doing that. He can get places without Stuyvesant.

Lucy: That's a hard thing to fight. There's a lot of status in being at Stuyvesant, and our whole society is geared to supporting you, saying you should. I'm having trouble with this example myself. Let me think about it a while and get back to you. We're not dealing with easy issues here. I don't have all the answers. Let's move away from competition as the opposite of cooperativism, and look more closely at signs of cooperativism itself.

One definition says cooperativism occurs when we work together to achieve our goals. I might say to you: "Carole, I can only succeed if you succeed." You might say to me: "Lucy, I can only succeed if you succeed." There are other expressions that convey cooperative thinking: "Our fates are linked." "We sink or we swim together." Can you think of other such statements?

Replies:

- We're all in the same boat.
- All for one, and one for all.
- One hand washes the other.
- A house divided against itself cannot stand.
- United we stand, divided we fall.
- Together we aspire, together we achieve.
- One hand cannot clap.

Lucy: Right, that's great. I know that you have had previous exposure to cooperativism from your religious and cultural backgrounds, which we should incorporate into our next in-service on this subject.

Our rewards, then, are based on our ability to perform well together. But we must not mistake cooperativism for altruism. Altruism is "unselfish interest in the welfare of others."

We are really almost selfish when we work cooperatively (not quite, though). We want to succeed ourselves, but we recognize that we can only succeed if we help one another. Researchers have called cooperativism a pragmatic strategy, which can lead to a happy work life, psychological health, and to our liking ourselves and others more (Kohn, 1986).

People who feel accepted by others, in cooperativism, also feel free and safe enough to explore problems more creatively, take risks, play with possibilities, and benefit from mistakes, rather than trying to endure in a competitive system in which mistakes must be hidden to avoid ridicule.

Like certain culturally determined attitudes, religious beliefs ought to play a role somewhere in our discussion, but right now, I am not sure exactly where—maybe I will be clearer about that after this introductory in-service. I first formed my ideas about COHME based on a cooperative agency my husband and I studied ten years ago in Bologna. The Catholic Church there had an important role in home care, and many of the aides came from a strong religious tradition. Right here in the United States, in this room in St. Elizabeth's Catholic Church, I know there are deeply religious people whose decision to enter this type of work was religiously motivated. Recently I visited a Baltimore home care agency, Bon Secours, founded in 1919 by French nuns, and their mission sounds in many ways like ours.

In COHME's cooperative, we have tried to have a democratic rather than a hierarchical organization of work. We have needed titles to be legally incorporated, but until fairly recently office staff, at least, have functioned with rather vague job descriptions—just everyone pitching in and doing the work that needed to be done. Decision making has been shared, and we reached a lot of decisions by consensus. Recently, in order to have greater efficiency, we've had to develop more policies and procedures. New York State Department of Health laws that have also required setting up rules that we cannot just refuse to obey or bring to you for an OK. Home health aides, in particular, must adhere to special state laws regarding their work and must attend at least twelve hours of in-services, like this one, every year. Still, in most instances, worker input is vital at COHME and carefully used. We would like you to speak up if you have any problems.

Now, I'm going to speak about some of COHME's successes and failures concerning cooperativism. When COHME first started, our office staff was composed of four highly intelligent, part-time, young high school graduates, who came from the same warm, close, extended religious family. (Many of you here probably remember these women.) I thought cooperativism was a breeze then, because these women had grown up together. They cooperated naturally. At that time some of our aides were friends of theirs, and they too were natural cooperators. These women told me that their cultural and religious backgrounds, economic realities, and other past experiences made them recognize the value of working together to achieve goals. I was, therefore, not prepared when, three years ago at a general meeting and in-service like this one, an angry aide stood up and screamed at me:

> So, we're all in this together? Well, my boss at COHME made me do windows, and that shouldn't be part of my job, but she still made me do it!

This woman had recently come to us from a highly exploitative working situation, where her professional home health aide skills weren't used, and where the only thing she did was housework, which included the hated washing of windows.

> "Who's your 'boss'?" asked a COHME veteran—a good question, since we don't use the term "boss," as you know.
> "Lucy!" the angry woman shouted. The COHME veteran said, laughingly: "Lucy made you do windows? You mean she beat you into doing it?"
> "No," said the woman, "but she was right there at the house, telling me, making me do it!"
> I had to break in. I said, "Where was I when I asked you to do the windows?" The new aide paused, then softly said, "Doing the windows."

I am trained as a home health aide as well as a social worker. When this new aide had been delayed getting to the case, our client was very upset. We had no other aide to replace her at the moment, so I went over to the client's apartment. This sick woman's only joy in life was looking out her window, which was filthy. I decided to start cleaning it, and was doing so when the delayed aide showed up. I cheerfully handed her another cloth, and we completed the window together. The aide was quiet. I was busy chatting with the client, and I never realized that the aide was so angry. She never questioned my actions at the time and never called me later at the office. She just let her anger and feelings of being exploited seethe inside her, until they exploded at a general meeting. At least she felt the safety and concern of her co-workers and was able to bring it up with the group. She sure let me have it! Actually, it was a great learning experience for all of us. The aide came to see that she was not being exploited, the other aides saw what exploitation can do to people, and I learned to explain what I was doing more carefully, and to look more closely for nonverbal communication signals shown by aides and staff.

There were a few more similar incidents, but with the help of our RNs, MSWs, and administrative staff, most aides' upsets that hindered their cooperative development were handled. We lost a few workers who found it impossible not to be competitive, but most aides fit very well into our cooperative system.

Then, our truly big problem began; we started having difficulties with our administrative office staff.

The jobs of the four part-time high school graduates who were running the office had to become full-time, and we required them to become involved with more specialized and sophisticated systems for scheduling, office management, and financial management. At one point, these women were staying at COHME until 1 and 2 a.m. to complete their work. When I found a partner in October 1989, we found a full-time administrative assistant, and these four loyal women gradually felt able to move on to less demanding positions. We tried briefly using aides to do office work since the administrative assistant needed help, and my partner needed to be out of the office, marketing. The aides tried, but they didn't like office work. They wanted to work with sick people. We realized that just as our aides—you—were special workers for the sick elderly in their homes, we needed more highly specialized people to work in the office. We began to hire college graduates with office experience and skills.

These new women in the office were more efficient; however, many had worked within the competitive system for many years where they were not well treated. They found it very hard to adapt to cooperativism. One woman hid her work, fearing a co-worker would find it and take credit from her. Another began to belittle aides and co-workers in the office and even became quite punitive. So many activities that we had previously all just pitched in and done together now required strict job descriptions so that no one would feel "dumped on." Some people deeply resented any late-nesses and were suspicious of explanations. Staff refused to make coffee or take turns taking out the trash.

I began to speculate about the psychological reasons for this behavior. For example, I was aware that some of these new women office workers had grown up in restrictive or oppressive family situations and wanted no reminder, through a cooperative work situation, of family-like relationships and obligations. Some were used to having power or having power imposed on them and now wanted to act powerfully with their co-workers. Some always had to put their personal needs before organizational needs, because they seemed to have had little nurturing in their lives. All these psychological factors, I thought, contributed to their behaving in this uncooperative, competitive way, but I was unable to change things. The tension in the office was becoming unbearable.

My partner and I finally called an emergency meeting of the board. We determined that some of our new staff were just not able to work cooperatively. When two highly competitive staff members were confronted by a board member with their behavior and with the need for them to change, both women immediately resigned in anger, left the office, and abandoned the rest of the staff to struggle together until replacements could be found.

So, these have been some of our successes and failures over the past six years. We have learned from our mistakes, I hope. I would now like to give you some examples of past competitive situations that we've tried to correct, cooperatively:

SITUATIONS TAKEN FROM AIDES' PROBLEMS

Example 1

Competitive Reaction: "The 8 p.m. aide is always late relieving me! I've been on this case twelve hours already, and I'm tired. She thinks she can waste my time. I'm not working with her anymore. She doesn't respect me. I have to pick up my kids and make dinner tonight. It's just too much!"

Cooperative Reaction: "I'm going to talk to my relief tonight and try to find out if she has subway or babysitter problems. Maybe we should adjust our hours. She's new to COHME; maybe she's not used to the way we do things. If I can't work it out with her, I'll tell the social worker. Maybe my relief will confide in the social worker."

Example 2

Competitive Reaction: "I do all the work during the day. She does nothing at night. It's not fair! Now, I have to go home and do all my own housework!"

Cooperative Reaction: "I'm going to chat with her tonight about this. Maybe we can distribute our tasks better. I know I just want to get things done fast. Maybe I don't give her enough of a chance. If my talking nicely to her doesn't work, I'll ask the COHME nurse to help or raise it myself at the next general meeting."

Example 3

Competitive Reaction: "That staff person in the office at COHME is so unreasonable! She won't let me change my schedule!"

Cooperative Reaction: "I guess I was so upset that I didn't explain my problem well enough to her. I know I've changed my schedule three times this month already, and it upsets my client, but my kids keep getting sick. Maybe I'll set up an appointment with a staff person and work this out. I'm so tired of rushing my kids and my husband out to get to work on time. Maybe I should switch to another case or see if the client could have me come later. Maybe a staff person could help me work this out—I'll ask her."

STAFF SITUATIONS IN THE OFFICE

Example 4

Competitive Reaction: "She came in late again! I get here on time; she just comes in whenever it suits her! I'm coming in late tomorrow!"

Cooperative Reaction: "I wonder if her hours are set like mine? Does she stay late a lot? If we need her to be here exactly on time, I'll raise having sign-in sheets at the next staff meeting. I wonder if her sister's sick again? I'll ask her about her sister."

Example 5

Competitive Reaction: "I'm exhausted! I've been trying to help this poor lady, but I can't get a good plan going!"

Cooperative Reaction: "Hey, why am I killing myself? We're all in this together! Why am I working on this alone? I'll get my co-workers and the MD involved. I can't save the world alone!"

I would like to make one more point before we start listing some more concrete definitions of cooperativism.

Aren't we really talking about women's issues here? Look at the examples I just gave: the need for babysitters, sick kids, rushing kids and husbands out in the morning, worrying about your own families and other women's families, picking up the kids, rushing home to make dinner, trying to get your own housework done.

Do most men talk like this and express having these problems? I don't think so. There are so many differences between men and women (Gilligan, 1982), differences that could make cooperation a natural thing for us if we women applied what we do in our family and personal relationships to what we do at work. Most women are interested in relationships, connection, and intimacy, the researchers tell us (Tannen, 1990). We know that! Most men, on the other hand, have traditionally been caught up with issues of status, independence, and, guess what?—competition. Recently, women have been encouraged in some quarters to become more competitive, but perhaps this behavior is really against our true natures. This does not mean that we women have to become wimps. What studies do show, however, is that women cherish friendship over competition. When little girls play a game, if there is disagreement about the rules, they will often start over or switch to another game. They do not want to risk losing a friendship over a game. We as women, then, need to continue challenging the competitive system and to reaffirm the importance of relationship, connection, and intimacy, not only in our personal lives but in our business lives as well.

As a cooperative, then, I would like to think that we women come to COHME because we are gifted at our work, we all need one another, we like the people we work with, we enjoy spending time with one another, and we have fun working on our cases together.

I guess I have gone back to some of the idealism expressed earlier in this in-service, which is OK, but now we have to get down to concrete, practical definitions of cooperativism, so we can teach it better to new and old aides, and so we can be guided as we hire new office staff. I'll list some of my ideas, in summary, then ask you for your ideas now, or you can send them into the COHME office, written out. Here are my summarized ideas:

First, COHME's cooperativism is nonprofit and noncompetitive; we work together to achieve our mission without making others fail or feel bad.

Second, COHME's cooperativism provides a democratic, non-hierarchical organization of work with most major decisions reached by consensus.

Third, COHME's cooperativism provides a friendly, nurturing, congenial atmosphere where workers feel free to express themselves; are not exploited; receive good pay, training, supervision, and counseling; have a high sense of self-esteem and good feelings about their co-workers; and like coming to work.

Fourth, COHME's cooperativism encourages creativity in work.

Fifth, COHME's cooperativism encourages the active participation of its board to enable us to better solve our problems. We subscribe to the old Chinese proverb: "Be secure enough to ask for help!"

Sixth, COHME's cooperativism encourages the attitude of having a "stake" in the agency, which will help us to move toward a guaranteed annual wage, health benefits, pensions, the worker/partner concept (which I haven't had time to discuss tonight), and other mutually beneficial goals.

Seventh, COHMEs cooperativism encourages doing our work for the betterment of our organization over doing work for personal gain, since we succeed individually only when the organization succeeds.

Now, what are your ideas?

REPLIES FROM EVERYONE
AT THE GENERAL MEETING

- The co-op should stand for teamwork.
- We should all feel we belong to a team.
- We should feel that we're all working together.
- The co-op should be sure everyone involved in a case knows everything that's going on in that case, especially the things that happen when the case ends.
- The co-op has to have good communications.
- Aides must take responsibility themselves to ask for any missing information, not just get upset when staff don't have all the answers—that's part of cooperativism.
- Staff need to "ask around" to get any needed information.
- Our co-op gives us these opportunities to let off steam; no one else has that, and you really listen to us.
- Other agencies don't provide a place where aides can regularly come and air their problems; that's very special, and I'm not sure people are aware of that.
- Most agencies don't give aides much information on the case before the aides go in.
- We want a secure, stable place to work.

Lucy: Great replies! It seems to me that your spontaneous comments and observations offer reason for hope that, with good will and equitable work relationships, cooperativism can succeed at COHME.

REFERENCES

Carpenter, Susan Streeter. (1990). "Profit Versus Non-profit: Comparisons and Considerations." *Home Health Care Nurse*, 4(1), pp. 18-23.

Gilligan, Carol. (1982). *In a Different Voice—Psychological Theory and Women's Development*, Cambridge, MA: Harvard University Press.

Kohn, Alfie. (1986). *The Case Against Competition—Why We Lose in Our Race to Win*, Boston: Houghton Mifflin Co.

Tannen, Deborah. (1990). *You Just Don't Understand—Women and Men in Conversation*, New York: William Morrow and Co.

PART III: USING COOPERATIVE STRATEGIES—SPECIALIZED TRAINING AND SUPERVISION OF HOME HEALTH AIDES

Because of its emphasis on cooperative strategies and comprehensive case management by social workers, registered nurses, and administrative staff, COHME began to get referrals that traditional agencies found difficult or not cost-effective. As a small, energetic agency, we turned no referral away, trusting that our particular skills and commitment would enable us to manage a difficult patient, such as a person with dementia, and that our creativity would help us discover ways to make small cases cost-effective through Cluster Care. These challenging cases required innovative training and daily supervision, since our aides were now functioning in emotionally demanding environments and had to acquire skills as "home managers" beyond their traditional home health care training.

The development of an in-service concerning racial issues was an especially sensitive undertaking. Part III gives examples of this and other types of training that COHME continues to offer its aides to enable them to function well in a cooperative environment. This training and supervision raised the self-esteem and status of COHME aides, which in turn enabled them to give better care to our most challenging clients.

Chapter 8

Training Aides to Care
for Dementia Clients

We have all seen situations in which home care workers are reluctant to call their agencies with a problem for fear that they will be seen as incapable of carrying out their functions. The message given, whether spoken or not, is, "Whatever the problem is, handle it yourself." We know that many situations in the care of elderly patients, particularly those with Alzheimer's disease, require aides to bring a lot of knowledge to the job and also to do a great deal of creative thinking to put that knowledge to effective use. But creative thinking ought to be a cooperative learning process in which aides can turn to their agency for help in their brainstorming efforts. We have a motto framed in our COHME office to encourage aides to turn to us: "Be secure enough to ask for help." This line of thinking was the impetus for the development of our unique Alzheimer's disease training course. Our workers become skilled in the management of even the most difficult behavioral problems of clients with Alzheimer's disease.

Some of our materials deal with defining dementia and the caregiver role, which help the worker to understand the stages through which both the client and their caregivers pass. Other materials help the workers with concrete steps in their attempts to manage behavioral problems. These in-services were originally one-on-one and focused on the client that the worker was currently seeing so that the worker went away with readily applicable knowledge. The

This chapter was written with Gertrude M. Smith, RN, C, and appeared in a longer version in *PRIDE Journal of Long Term Home Health Care*, 9(2), Spring 1990, pp. 56-59.

worker had an opportunity to raise questions and review material that was relevant to his or her client and his or her own knowledge base, and to obtain emotional support. The in-service was used even with new COHME workers. We recognized how fortunate we were at COHME to be able to conduct our training in such an ideal way.

As the agency grew, however, such individualized training became impossible. We had videotaped a dynamic presentation dealing factually and emotionally with the agitated client with Alzheimer's disease. We began using this tape with a small group of workers, and it became evident that the workers were learning from one another as well as from the tape. Additionally, they were enjoying the rare opportunity of sharing their caregiving experiences with their colleagues. Newer workers were learning from more experienced workers in a setting we were able to monitor. Here was a chance to allow our workers to share techniques and experiences while still providing an educational structure.

We decided to expand this group experience by developing an educational curriculum for our workers that would include their own as well as their clients' emotional needs. Thus a curriculum developed that we hoped would provide:

1. a concrete educational structure dealing with the demented client;
2. a format in which workers shared and participated in their own professional growth as well as in that of their colleagues;
3. an opportunity for workers to learn more about themselves and their feelings and to be able to use this knowledge in their job setting; and
4. some instruction in stress-reduction techniques.

The curriculum ran for six sessions. It was jointly led by a social worker and the nurse who developed the curriculum. Each session featured an educational topic such as behavioral changes in persons suffering from Alzheimer's disease. Enough time was left for the aides to vent their emotional concerns related to this specific educational content. Each class consisted of a mix of experienced and inexperienced workers. A pretest was developed that pulled relevant questions from our previously taught individual in-services, as well as questions that would help the workers begin focusing on feelings. The videotape constituted the core of two of the sessions, while it provided the workers with a take-off point for discussion of their own immediate problems and successes with particular clients.

Presently we are about to begin our third group and are learning with every session. The first group taught us to expect the unexpected. The pressure to speak and to be heard was palpable and was something we had not foreseen. For those workers it was enough just to be together. They were more than ready to share experiences and our session structure simply got in the way of this process. We had to adjust our format to allow for their needs and we found that flexibility on the part of the leaders was vital. The overall goals of the curriculum remain unchanged, but, clearly, the structure will undergo continual reevaluation and revision.

We have found the pretest to be a vital springboard that allows the workers to try untested waters and often gain validation from their co-workers. One question deals with distancing and gives a scenario of a patient with clearly worsening dementia.

Pretest Question

You have been caring for a patient whose condition has worsened to the point where he or she mixes you up with other people. You feel:

1. hurt because the patient doesn't remember you;
2. closer to the patient;
3. sad because the job isn't the same anymore; or
4. distanced from the patient due to the progress of the illness.

Several of the workers saw themselves as growing closer to their clients during this time. "They need me more" was among the reasons given.

Some workers reported that for a while they had unconsciously imitated some of their patients' characteristics. "I forget things!"

Others put up with abusive situations because they felt that they were expected to and were relieved to hear their co-workers (and us) tell them that these were not situations that needed to be tolerated.

We have also found the combination of the RN and MSW very valuable because each one brings a slightly different slant to the session and the problem solving that goes on within it. The RN and MSW have gained a new respect for the work that we ask these caregivers to perform.

While we are still committed to our original curriculum concepts, we continue to make adjustments and will continue to do so as the needs of the workers arise. We are, after all, dealing with the most demanding clients of all, and adaptability is the name of the game!

Chapter 9

Training Aides
to Work in Cluster Care
with the Newly Dependent Elderly

As America grays, and with the elderly over age eighty-five now representing the fastest growing segment of our population (U.S. Bureau of the Census, 1990), more home health aides will be needed to provide competent care to dependent seniors. Dependency, however, is a complex issue, and training aides to work with this population is a difficult task.

The purpose of this chapter is twofold: (1) to briefly discuss the concept of dependency and (2) to present the text of a training program that was designed and used by the authors to facilitate the resolution of problems which emerged when Cluster Care was introduced into a home care agency and implemented in a senior residence. The text can be used to train home health aides who will be working within a Cluster Care format for the first time.

DEPENDENCY

Elderly persons who suffer an acute health crisis—falling and fracturing a hip and requiring hospitalization, for example—cannot deny the need for home aide assistance. They are definitely dependent. The inability to walk, prepare meals, bathe, or perform other necessary activities of daily living make home aides needed assistants, and usually the service is gratefully accepted by elderly clients. However, when elderly individuals are just beginning to become dependent—perhaps

Written with Friedhilde Milburn, CSW, and Maura Ryan, RN, C, PhD, GNP. This chapter was originally published in *Home Health Care Nurse*, Fall, 1996, pp. 638-646.

forgetting to eat or bathe regularly, to clean their homes or apartments well, occasionally leaving pots on the stove to burn, or in other ways endangering their well-being—there is often quite a different response. Elders can often "catch" themselves and repair the damage, even correct unusual behavior when a significant other comments on negative changes of habit. They may cover up beginning deficits with a quick distracting story, charming excuse, or even by withdrawing from social contacts that may expose their deficits. Most elderly people fear aging, memory loss, disability, and dependency. Accepting aide help in our "rugged individual" culture frequently means "having one foot in the grave." It is easy, therefore, to understand the desire of these elders to deny both impairment and the need for assistance. The authors will refer to this second group of impaired seniors as the "newly dependent" elderly.

Until recently, newly dependent elderly have been an ill-defined and difficult-to-serve population. Initiatives have begun, within the New York City Medicaid home care system and within a few other nursing and social service agencies, to institute a service delivery system called Cluster Care or Shared Aide Program to help these elderly clients.

Cluster Care enables a cognitively aware elderly person to utilize a minimum number of aide hours because the aide is shared with others who require assistance and who live in the same building or nearby. Cluster Care is, therefore, less expensive and less invasive of privacy, since an aide is only present when tasks need to be done. There are confidentiality issues and burn-out possibilities for the aide, and anxiety and jealousy issues for the client, but good social work and nursing case management can usually minimize these problems.

Using the Cluster Care format, the authors implemented this specialized, limited home care model using their agencies: James Lenox House, a senior apartment residence of "seemingly independent" elderly in Manhattan, and COHME. After legal and contractual arrangements were in place, the negotiation and introduction of the new program was handled through separate and combined meetings with administrators, social workers, and home health aides in both agencies. Soon after Cluster Care was introduced into the residence, problems began to present themselves for both aides and newly dependent clients. Aides were often too invested in their traditional home health aide training to be effective working with these "closeted" newly dependent elderly. COHME prided itself on caring for older adults who had difficult physical and emotional problems, particularly Alzheimer's disease, where the judgments of the clients were poor, and the aides were forced to make most of the day-to-day decisions to keep them safe at home. For their part, the residence clients were too invested in denying disability and maintaining their image of independence. They preferred to choose housekeepers whose low cost and lack of home care training enabled them to pretend that they had no serious need for help.

As discussed earlier in this chapter, with the onset or exacerbation of a medical illness or the crisis of a fall, especially if it required hospitalization, these elderly residents would generally accept the temporary placement of a home health aide, especially if the aides were covered by the Medicare program and their services did not cost the residents money. Even during these brief periods, however, residents tended to become upset, feeling that their homes were being invaded and their privacy lost. When the Medicare program ended, the residents often tried to return to a now very inappropriate housekeeper level of help. At this point, the director of the residence and her staff usually advised the residents to accept privately paid home health aides to maintain their rehabilitation gains. Given the additional cost and the presence of an undeniable paraprofessional level of care entering the home of the residents, the situation became very difficult for the elderly clients to handle and presented a major challenge to the home health aides and their supervisors. A decision was reached by both agencies to plan and implement a training program for the home health aides, which would provide anticipatory guidance and smooth the transition to Cluster Care.

TRAINING AIDES TO CARE
FOR THE NEWLY DEPENDENT ELDERLY

The residence's social work staff continued the traditional counseling needed to help these newly dependent elderly begin to accept their disabilities and their need for home health aides. Meanwhile, the home care agency worked together with the residence director to formally create a new in-service training course for the home health aides. The residence director served as course instructor, the residence nurse practitioner acted as advisor, and COHME's director created and edited the course content with a view to future publication. The resulting course was titled: "How to Work with Newly Dependent Elderly Clients in Cluster Care Home Care." The objectives of the training course were to:

1. sensitize competent home health aides to the special needs of this newly dependent elderly population; and
2. instruct aides on specific strategies and guidelines to defuse the denial and resistance of their clients to their interventions.

An edited transcript of remarks made by the residence instructor at a videotaped in-service program given to COHME's home health aides follows. The training took place next door to COHME in the local church basement, a spacious, comfortable room frequently rented by COHME for large aide training programs. Beverages were served beforehand, and a relaxed, informal atmosphere was fostered. Participation by members of the group was encouraged. They enthusiastically shared both some of their experiences in caring for their clients and the manner in which they solved some of the problems that they had encountered. Excerpts from the training program are presented here. It is the intent of the authors that the vignettes serve as a useful guide to aides and supervisors working with this frail, newly dependent population.

EDITED TEXT OF IN-SERVICE PROGRAM: RESIDENCE DIRECTOR'S REMARKS TO HOME HEALTH AIDES

Our James Lenox House residents range in age from 55 to 103; most are over 85. They are primarily middle-class, retired business, professional, and service people, and predominantly women. At any given time, 30 to 40 percent need some help beyond that of a housekeeper, but they can't think of their help as being too "professional" in the traditional sense of a home health aide. They have had accidents in the past—a broken leg, a broken hip. They become forgetful. Complications of their chronic medical conditions necessitate trained aide care.

These impaired elderly realize that they cannot burden the residence staff too much, nor can they rely too heavily on their family, neighbors, or friends. They must turn to you, but for you to be successful with this type of client, it becomes necessary to combine your traditional aide training with flexibility and intuition. You, who have worked hard to become home health aides and may plan to become licensed practical nurses or registered nurses in the future, must now modify the manner in which you deliver care. To be successful with our population of newly dependent elderly who are very busy denying their dependency and guarding their privacy, appearing too traditionally "professional" in the sense of taking charge may be perceived as a threat. Let me explain this statement more carefully.

It is sometimes helpful in our work to think about your own home. Suppose you came home today to start dinner, and you saw all your appliances, pots, pans, and dishes rearranged according to the latest model of domestic efficiency. Your husband, boyfriend, child, friend, or another significant other just went into your kitchen and did it. They did not consult with you beforehand, because a TV expert had said that this was the best way to arrange a modern kitchen and your loved one or helper wanted the best for you. Oh, and while your helper was rearranging your kitchen, he had also turned the dial of your radio station from "lite" FM to heavy metal, so that when you came home, rushing in with packages to prepare dinner, and quickly flipped on your radio, you were assaulted by outrageously loud sounds coming from this kitchen that you didn't recognize. You'd be pretty upset, confused, and angry, wouldn't you?

This is exactly how our residents feel when you change things so they are "better," more efficient, and safer under your value system or under rules you were taught in school in order to become a home health aide. Actually, there is no single way to do most things. You, I, and your clients come from varied backgrounds and have different habits and expectations. As the aides of our residents, you must recognize, learn, and respect their norms. When you enter their homes, you enter their turf.

It is also probably better not to label them "dependent"—try to think of them as older people who need help. People with hip fractures are not Alzheimer's disease clients. They are angry when you move their personal articles around or make decisions without consulting them. The visiting nurse's suggestion that the scatter rugs be removed infuriates them and they resist vehemently. They love these rugs, the apartment looks bare without them, they promise to be careful and not slip on them *again!* So, even though the rugs were responsible for a hip fracture, clients can't bear to change the furnishings in the apartment.

Now, here is where your home health aide training comes in. They are not safe with these rugs the way they are. Some of you might know that there is a special tape that you can put under these rugs that will prevent skidding. They will probably accept your making this change for safety, but if not, you can talk to the nurses and social workers at your home care agency or at the residence, and ask for their assistance. They will work with the elderly client to make the needed change happen without jeopardizing your relationship. Use your colleagues. As a general rule, in any case, *increase your network*. Among the various disciplines and individuals involved, choose the discipline or individual who generates the least resistance from your client to help you. This might be a maintenance person, the in-house beautician, the office secretary, a religious confidant, a family member, or even legal counsel.

Although your home care agency will generally orient you to whatever the home health care needs of your clients are, we at the residence will inform you about particularly difficult issues for specific clients, what has worked in the past, what has not, and introduce you to them.

The residence's clients are very sensitive to the tone of your voice. If you say: "I would like to please you by knowing what you like" in a tone that clearly says: "You're driving me crazy with your silly demands!" they will perceive the incongruity and become uncooperative. You may be anxious yourself, but remember, they are anxious too. You are a new person coming into the sanctity of their homes and interfering in their lives.

CLUSTER CARE CONFIDENTIALITY

Two of the greatest advantages of Cluster Care are: (1) it enables newly dependent elderly to become less resistant to accepting help, since they can have the number of hours they can tolerate or find definite tasks for you to perform in a short time; (2) it enables you to have a full day's work (often a problem in the home care industry) since you have several clients for short hours.

Confidentiality is always an important issue but especially in a situation where you are affiliated with several clients in the same residence. Mrs. T. may say: "I know you're visiting Mrs. R. How is she?" or "So, Mrs. R. is using you, too. She has lots of money to pay you, right? Did her son give it to her?" The temptation here is to call on your traditional training and perhaps give the client a gentle ethics lecture. The better reaction is: "Mrs. T., with all respect, I'm sure you wouldn't like me to share your business with others, so I don't want to tell anyone else's either. I'm sure you understand. By the way, perhaps Mrs. R. would enjoy a visit or call from you."

COMPASSION

We all try to be compassionate, but our clients at times can upset us greatly. Sometimes we need to put up a kind of "mental screen" to protect ourselves. We can see through the screen, but the client's angry responses do not directly touch us. We don't react defensively to a difficult request. It is difficult but useful to consider the situation as an opportunity to grow as a home care provider.

The "mental screening" process usually follows a pattern of "self talk." Ask yourself Why is Mrs. M. treating me this way? Then, tell yourself:

1. I am a trained home health aide; she is ill and my client; I'm not going to take it personally.
2. *But,* my approach will in no way be condescending or patronizing; I'll be charitable and compassionate.
3. If I feel overwhelmed and not sure I can trust the "mental screen," I will call my supervisor or the residence social worker/nurse/director.

I would now like us to develop vignettes or concise stories from our collective home care experiences to illustrate the points that I've already discussed with you.

(The following vignettes are the highly conceptualized results of an interactive teaching process. The instructor, along with the RNs and MSWs in the audience, carefully teased out the salient points in each aide's discussion of her relationship with her client. The vignettes were then edited. It is suggested that instructors encourage aide participants, after hearing or reading these vignettes, to develop stories from their own personal home care experiences, stressing that there is no expectation that these new stories will be polished presentations.)

EDITED VIGNETTES: BREAKING THE ICE AND INTRODUCING TECHNIQUES

Resident Mrs. A. is a retired secretary, who likes to communicate in writing to hide a hearing problem. When anyone speaks to her, she pretends to understand and nods. She realizes she appears stupid, becomes frustrated and angry, and withdraws. She does not answer her phone because she cannot hear but refuses hearing devices. She is becoming more isolated. With illness, an aide is needed and is engaged. The residence's nurse introduces the aide, modeling the behavior she would like the new aide to adopt. She sits close to Mrs. A. and speaks directly to her in a low voice register, which is more easily heard. She engages her in small talk. She brings the aide over to where she is sitting. The aide, in conservative street clothes, takes the nurse's seat. Calmly and with a smile, the aide asks slowly and clearly if she could make Mrs. A. a cup of tea. Mrs. A. smiles in return and accepts.

Resident Mr. M.'s air conditioner broke down on Friday at 5:30 p.m., and it was very hot in his apartment. The residence staff had left for the weekend. His experienced aide, who knew the building well, was to leave at 5:30 p.m. but stayed late, went to three apartments, and borrowed fans. When Mr. M. was more comfortable and emergency services had been notified of the need to repair his air conditioner, the aide left.

Resident Dr. P. is very frail and has aide help only during the day, but wanders at night. The night doorman at the residence distracts her and is able to talk her into returning to her apartment. During the day, Dr. P. is not so distracted. Her aide walks behind her, not offering her an arm but staying close enough to catch her, if needed. Her pocketbook dangles dangerously on her arm, but the aide simply walks close enough for would-be thieves to know Dr. P. is not alone. In the drugstore, Dr. P. asks for hairspray, and becomes frustrated when the clerk asks for the brand. She turns to the aide: "What do you use?" The aide draws Dr. P.'s attention to all the brands on a shelf and vaguely points. Dr. P. visually recognizes her usual spray and buys it. On the way out, exhausted, Dr. P. puts her hand through the aide's arm. Neither says anything about this; they just discuss the traffic on the way back home.

The Cluster Care aide feels very concerned that Mr. R. will only accept her two hours a day. Mr. R. drops lots of items and breaks them, occasionally soils himself, and sometimes soils the apartment. The residence social worker explains that Mr. R. will not tolerate more hours of help; she feels everyone must accept the need for a lesser level of care for this gentleman. The home care agency nurse is concerned about safety and hygiene issues, such as Mr. R.'s injuring himself on broken glass, falling on a soiled floor, or getting skin breakdown (a deterioration caused by the skin's prolonged contact with urine and feces). The residence social worker negotiates a compromise—breakable items will be removed from the apartment daily; the aide will clean up messes as long as they only occur occasionally, and the nurse will visit more often to assess skin breakdown.

Mrs. B. accepted an aide only to please her family. The first day, she sat reading and told the aide to just sit. The aide asked if she could read too. They started discussing books and magazine articles. On the second day, while both sat reading, the aide said with a big smile: "Isn't there something you'd love to have me do for you today, your way of course?" The aide felt she'd given Mrs. B. "the upper hand." Mrs. B. let her make dinner, the client's way.

It was Mr. S.'s first day with help, and the aide's first day with the agency. Both parties were nervous, anxious, and suspicious. There was a sudden worsening of Mr. S.'s medical condition, and the aide supervised Mr. S.'s transfer to the hospital. While he was being examined, the aide bought a get well balloon and presented it to Mr. S., who cried and grabbed her hand.

Mrs. U., with severe leg ulcers, yelled at the aide from her seat: "Get away; I don't need you! Leave!" The aide went into another room and peeped in at Mrs. U. at intervals, showing herself but saying nothing. Mrs. U. had to urinate, and kept struggling to get up. The aide was careful not to watch Mrs. U. during the struggle itself. Finally, Mrs. U. was exhausted and said, "Aren't you going to help me?" The aide said nothing, got up, and helped Mrs. U. Later the aide told the social worker, "It was a difficult experience for me. I got a strain in my neck from all that peeping, but it was worth it. She loves me now!"

The registered nurse and the physician wanted Mrs. A. to use a medication box to help her remember to take her pills at the proper times and to ensure proper dosage. Mrs. A. told the daily aide: "If I've come to the state that I need a box, may God take me!" The aide worked with Mrs. A. The aide displayed all the medicine bottles while she was on duty and Mrs. A. took appropriate medication out of the bottles, for then and for later that night. The aide then hid the bottles, leaving the night medication with Mrs. A.'s note, "These meds need be taken at 8 p.m."

Mrs. C. learned her aide's favorite television soap opera and suggested they sit together and watch it. Mrs. C. then complained to the residence director that the aide did no work, just watched TV. The home care agency social worker made a home visit at the aide's request. Mrs. C. explained that they both relaxed and chatted together as they watched TV, but since the aide was a guest in her home, they watched the aide's program. The aide was shocked and said it was important to watch Mrs. C.'s program. The aide would tape her soap opera at home.

Mrs. E. thought her bank was burning down and wanted to see it at 2 a.m. The night aide had the doorman call a car service known to the residence, got in with Mrs. E., and locked all the doors for security. They drove by the bank and, seeing it intact, Mrs. E. was reassured. They drove back home, and Mrs. E. slept well the rest of the night. The aide later informed the home care social worker, who called Mrs. E.'s psychiatrist, who changed her night medications.

Miss V. used her Cluster Care aide from 12 noon to 3:30 p.m., insisting that the aide "disappear" exactly at 3:30 p.m. She invited guests in for tea almost every afternoon at 4 p.m., feeling secure that none of her friends knew how dependent she was on the aide to produce this satisfying social event.

Instructor's Remarks

This was a lively and informative development of vignettes, which I hope you found helpful and useful for your future work with this challenging Cluster Care population of newly dependent elderly. Since this in-service is being videotaped it will be available for future sessions and for your colleagues who were unable to attend today's training session. Let me express my gratitude for your excellent ideas and full participation.

CONCLUSIONS

Although COHME and James Lenox House initially invested considerable time and expense in the case management needed for setting up Cluster Care clients, within one to two months home care for each resident became quite cost-effective for both agencies. Appropriate aides were then in place and accepted, and the assessments and care plans were developed and put into effect.

Not all home care aides can adapt to Cluster Care work. Some feel very disoriented, moving from client to client, and need routine functions with the same client every day. In contrast, some aides relish the unexpected, the variety, and the more rapid pace associated with Cluster Care. They like getting to know the whole residence staff, and enjoy meeting other residents over tea, at the laundry, or at the supermarket. It may take a few false starts before a home care agency finds the cadre of workers best suited for Cluster Care.

The work of a home health aide can be frustrating, especially when dealing with newly dependent elderly clients who are denying their losses and detesting the fact that they need aide help. The work can also be rewarding when aides use both traditional home health aide skills and their own flexibility, intuition, and good sense. The short in-service course described in this chapter documents some of the know-how necessary to do this challenging job. Videos have also been a useful new training tool to help aides and clients develop trusting relationships within Cluster Care arrangements (COHME/JLH, 1993; and see Chapter 10).

As we move into the twenty-first century, with a projected 20 percent of our population over 65 and less than 5 percent in nursing homes, more and more skilled aides will be needed to keep the elderly safe at home. If we can enable newly dependent elderly to accept help before a crisis occurs by modifying our traditional attitudes and approaches toward appropriate home health aide training and care, we may eliminate many falls and exacerbations of chronic illness. We may also help keep the elderly more independent for a longer period of time. We certainly would be contributing to a much healthier old-old age for this population.

REFERENCES

COHME/JLH. (1993). *How to Develop Trusting Relationships Between Home Care Clients and Home Care Workers.* Lucy Rosengarten, ACSW and Friedhilde Milburn, CSW. Video.

United States Bureau of the Census. (1990). *Statistical Abstracts of the United States,* 108th Edition. Washington, DC: U.S. Government Printing Office.

Chapter 10

Developing Trusting Relationships Between White Clients and Black Aides

At a Group Work Symposium, COHME and James Lenox House presented a video demonstrating beginning group work efforts to help frail, white, female elderly, and their black, female home care aides better understand their common problems and their need for developing trust in one another. The results of the video and the symposium group discussion that followed influenced future Cluster Care work between the two agencies.

For several years COHME had occasionally provided short-term aide help to seniors at James Lenox House when they were temporarily ill following hospitalization or a sudden at-home illness. The group leaders had worked well together on the needed assessments and care plans for these short-term home care services and had served together on various geriatric projects and committees within their larger Manhattan community. Both social workers regularly employed group work methods within their own agencies.

It therefore became a natural extension of the leaders' previous work together to use group work processes to address one of the most difficult barriers to maintaining frail elderly people safely at home—the lack of trust between white elderly and their black aides. The leaders felt that the production of a video in which both the white elderly and their black aides frankly discussed their perceptions of one another would be helpful in planning future Cluster Care work together.

This chapter was originally presented with Friedhilde Milburn, CSW, at a Group Work Symposium sponsored by the Association for the Advancement of Social Work with Groups, New York City, October 1993.

Each author first ran her own taped group within her own agency. Both groups were inexpensively videotaped, giving six aides in one group and four elderly in the other group an opportunity to get used to the format and the technology within their familiar agency settings and with trusted leaders. The starting goal of the authors was clearly spelled out within each of the individual meetings: the eventual joining together of individuals from the two groups in order to begin joint discussions of how to develop trusting relationships between them. The individual groups thus had opportunities to formulate and conceptualize their concerns within their own agency's protective setting. The home care nursing manager co-led in the COHME home care group to give additional support and security to the aides. The elderly James Lenox House residents were reassured in their individual session by the presence of a residence board member, a retired film producer who served as technical advisor to the entire project. The same video technician taped all of the videos.

Three individuals from each group were selected for the decisive interactive video. They met together at the residence to form a new group of six. No COHME aide knew any of the residence participants. Name tags and seating directions were considered by the group leaders but finally rejected because the leaders felt that such a method would be perceived as too controlling and too detail oriented. They wanted to minimize the tension of a stressful encounter with the video camera. Having left seating to random selection, the COHME group leader landed in the middle of the three James Lenox House residents, two of whom she knew from other meetings. The residence group leader landed on the end of the semi-circle, next to the three aides, whom she welcomed warmly to this new setting. Taping went more smoothly than anticipated, eliciting spirited discussion after some initial nervous hesitation.

The group leaders had planned to edit all three videos to present at this symposium; however, it became clear that time and financial constraints made major editing impossible. The group leaders, therefore, decided to edit only the third interactive video, which fortunately contained several references to the earlier two videos, especially the important theme of "mutual concerns." At the symposium presentation, the leaders decided, they could fill in any other needed information from the two earlier videos.

At the symposium, the lively discussion by social workers right after the showing of the video helped the leaders learn about other similar projects. They received immediate feedback and information to further advance their thinking about the future of these groups, including their usefulness in Cluster Care work.

RESULTS OBTAINED FROM THE VIDEOTAPE

The taped group of white residents and black aides together showed that despite cultural differences they had many concerns in common: racism, inadequate health care, family issues, finances, religion, women's issues, ageism, self-acceptance, housing concerns, crime, and violence. The residents, in addition, expressed concern about dependency and illness. The aides, in addition, expressed concerns about unemployment and showed signs of low self-esteem.

Aides, realistically describing their past effective methods of coping with distrust on the part of their elderly clients, reported using techniques of confrontation, avoidance, ignoring, denial, minimization, acceptance, humor, distancing, professionalism, ventilation, patience, discussion, and calling on trusted agency professionals. They usually reported good results, with client trust toward them developing over time. There was no mention of the aides trusting the clients, but one sensed a "calling" to this work, which encouraged their own trust.

Residents, describing in a genteel manner their past experiences with aides, reported needing time to adjust to the aide's presence and cultural differences. They accepted help when the trusted residence social work leader vouched for the aide. There was a denial of personal prejudices, especially racial, and general intellectualizing. Great curiosity and interest were expressed, and questions were asked about the past home care experiences of the aides.

SYMPOSIUM DISCUSSION

As part of the lively professional group discussion that followed the taped group presentation at the symposium, the home care leader reported that her earlier aide tape was more blunt and direct, especially about the racial prejudice aides experience. The residence leader, on the other hand, reported that her earlier tape showed even more denial of racial prejudices than when the residents were together with the aides.

The presenters explained that tape editing made the entire joint group seem more articulate than they were and that, in reality, much confusing group process was lost on the cutting room floor. Also, with a more sophisticated taping system, more nonverbal reactions would have been picked up. The COHME presenter observed her own angry facial expressions and body language in response to one of her worker's comments. This opportunity for self-observation makes taping an excellent learning tool for group workers. The residence presenter's facial expressions were lost in profile seating, although her expressive body language was observable. The COHME presenter had to introduce the topic of race, but once it was presented, there was a beginning of joint discussion and a recognition of the mutual problem, which was an advance over the resident tape.

The experienced, professional group workers at the symposium spoke about the significance of group selection and the greater coping and learning abilities of these aides, who had high school educations, home health aide certificates, and good in-service training, supervision, and agency support. The residents also benefited from good educations, adequate health status, and some financial resources.

The presenters then discussed their plan to continue these groups on a monthly basis as part of a new Cluster Care contract between their two agencies. They predicted the ongoing groups would be well accepted, since everyone involved had a good time participating in these groups. It had already become a status symbol within both agencies to have been "in on" the video. There seemed to be a relief and a release in having this somewhat glamorous film format in which each group expressed to the other previously unmentioned issues. Perhaps the frank afternoon television talk shows that both groups watch made it easier for participants to begin to express long-concealed emotions. Even the video technician, a young, black male actor and filmmaker, told the group his mother had been a home aide, and he recalled the many indignities she had suffered from her white employers. All participants enjoyed contributing to the educational symposium and received copies of the tape. The person-to-person communication networks are strong in each agency, and word is out that a new, exciting program is in the offing, and they will all be part of it.

CONCLUSIONS

Although the COHME/James Lenox House Cluster Care concept was a more affordable, more efficient way to deliver home health care services to this newly dependent elderly population and benefited both groups greatly, barriers to utilizing these services effectively developed due to a lack of trust between the frail white elderly women and their black home health aides. Beginning group work efforts uncovered prejudices on both sides, along with the realization, however, that as women and as sometimes marginalized members of society, they had more in common than was first evident in their racial and cultural differences. After the first meeting, the two directors noted a positive direction in both groups toward developing mutual trust but recognized that at least monthly joint group meetings would be needed at James Lenox House to effect real change and lead to the Cluster Care program's success. Having the directors of both agencies lead the groups increased both the aides' and the clients' motivation to attend.

The use of the video camera produced better than expected results, since both groups were fond of the television talk show format and were comfortable with being taped. In addition, receiving copies of the videotape helped reinforce the importance of this group work, as all the women showed the tape to their friends and co-workers. Ongoing group work efforts would not require this continuous incentive. However, a one-shot financial investment to produce a demonstration tape is recommended.

Cluster Care gives elderly white clients exactly the number of hours of aide help that they really need, while having a few low-hour clients gives the health care worker full employment. Given the fact that most home health care workers in New York City are black, confronting racial prejudices is a prerequisite for a successful home care plan.

REFERENCE

James Lenox House/COHME, Inc. (1993, October). "How to Develop Trusting Relationships Between Home Care Clients and Home Care Workers." All rights reserved. To obtain this video contact: Friedhilde Milburn, CSW, James Lenox House, 49 E. 73rd St., New York, NY 10021 or Lucy Rosengarten, CSW, COHME, Inc., 157 East 86th St., 3rd floor, New York, NY 10028.

PART IV: COHME'S APPROACH TO GERIATRIC CASE MANAGEMENT

In the spring of 1988, I was delighted when professors at the University of Indiana invited me to participate in the creation of a training manual for Medicaid case managers in their state. The reason for my delight was that the type of work we had been doing at COHME since 1985 with a middle-class clientele and small caseloads was being seen by academic specialists in the field as relevant not only to people who could afford our services but also to Medicaid clients. I began to realize that certain aspects of COHME's unique case management could also be applicable to poor families struggling to obtain services within the Medicaid system. As in Bologna, where the city government adopted some of the methods of CADIAI (see Chapter 6) to improve their home care system, here in the United States a group of academics in Indiana were asking COHME to enhance the training in-service manual used by Medicaid line workers.

Later in 1988, I received another validating request, this time to teach a course for Medicaid case managers working at a senior housing center in a poor Hispanic community in East Harlem. And four years later, in 1992, I was asked to summarize the results of that course for another group of Medicaid caseworkers at a two-day seminar held at Rockefeller College in New York City.

The responses to the article and to the two presentations were quite gratifying. As the reader will see in Chapter 12, I focused attention in my case management teaching on the One-Sheet, which the Medicaid workers in East Harlem eventually found useful.

It has always been a problem to present social work home care case management in a concise form that will be read by other professionals and that can be taught to social workers, some of whom may not have the benefits of an MSW. It is also important to present social work case management in a manner that legislators can understand, so that in the future it will become a reimbursable service.

Chapter 11

Principles of COHME's Case Management

Case management is a complex problem-solving process whose purpose is to obtain, integrate, and coordinate social, psychological, and health services for needy individuals and their families. This process involves a series of interrelated procedures, which are described later in this chapter.

Although exceptional laypeople are able to coordinate these diverse services, in general the day-by-day process of case management is a task best performed by trained social workers, representatives of the formal system who work in concert with informal networks of family and friends. Informal networks provide a great deal of supportive case management services and, ideally, work in tandem with the professional case manager.

As a specialized area of professional competence, case management evolved during the 1960s along with many other social and health service programs then emerging throughout the United States. The need for such specialization arose when it became clear that the rapid proliferation of these programs resulted in a fragmented and inefficient delivery system. Concerned governmental programs (such as Medicare and Medicaid) created specific positions called case managers in order to place the responsibility for providing needed social and health services within one locus of control. During the 1970s, these integrative initiatives developed

This chapter first appeared in a different form, in a training manual on aging and disability for Medicaid Workers, published by Indiana University Press. *Aging and Developmental Disabilities—A Training In-Service Package Module 5.A*, ed. Barbara A. Hawkins, (Bloomington, IN: 1989), pp. 5-28.

into full governmental case management programs and services for numerous populations.

Many people in this country have a severely critical view of all large bureaucracies; however, a great deal of creative thinking and organizational skills went into the original development of these programs, including case management programs.

Today, of course, the political climate is very different from that of the 1960s. Resources are far more limited, and governmental case management services are not as available as they were. This has encouraged the growth of voluntary, nongovernmental agencies as well as of private practitioners specializing in case management. Because of the variety of its roles and functions, and the many different kinds of agencies involved, case management has taken on somewhat different meanings and connotations within various types of agencies. As a consequence of this diversification, controversies outlined later in this chapter have arisen as to who is best suited to perform case management and what services should be included in the concept.

GERIATRIC CASE MANAGEMENT

Geriatric case management is the same comprehensive coordinated service described above, provided by a variety of professionals and nonprofessionals. It is specifically intended to help only frail or sick elderly and their families, and its goals can include the following:

1. Helping the elderly to remain safely, independently, and happily within their own homes and communities for as long as possible
2. Helping the elderly and their families to cope with transitions to more dependent status when needed (e.g., living with a family member or aide on a part-time or full-time basis; accepting nutritional and health care interventions; assisting with finances, transportation, etc.)
3. Helping those elderly and their families who need to consider a move to a more protected living environment, such as senior housing, enriched housing, a continuing care facility, or a nursing home

4. Helping the elderly and their families cope with client/patient physical and mental deterioration, dying, and death

RANGE OF SERVICES PROVIDED BY PROFESSIONAL GERIATRIC CASE MANAGERS

Assessment

The first step in making a professional assessment is to gather information that identifies the strengths and weaknesses of the elderly client/patient's present medical and psychiatric condition and functional capacities. Such information is obtained through interviews conducted with clients/patients, their families and friends, and involved professionals. These interviews take place in hospitals, homes, or on the telephone. The purpose of the interviews is to determine many diverse aspects of the elderly individual's life situation. Among the crucial areas of concern are the following:

1. Level of disability
2. Current and past illnesses
3. Present emotional state
4. Event(s) precipitating case manager involvement
5. Past history of coping abilities
6. Formal system support (hospital, doctor, senior center, bank, postal worker, clergy)
7. Informal system support (family, friends, neighbors, doorman, grocer, etc.)
8. Economic status
9. Living arrangements
10. Interests
11. Personal appearance

After concluding the information-gathering and interviewing process (see the case study later in this chapter, which calls this "identifying information"), the case manager proceeds with the crucial task of interpreting the data, which is the true assessment. *This is the most important aspect of case management, for without this interpretation, the case manager cannot go on to produce an effective plan.*

Making a skilled assessment requires professional social work training; it is an analytical process that incorporates physical, psychological, social, and cultural aspects of the individual's life. The interpretation is usually elaborated in a narrative account, weaving the identifying data into coherent explanations and evaluations.*

The Treatment Plan

Producing a treatment plan involves making creative use of the assessment to provide an appropriate array of activities and services for needy clients/patients and their families. Treatment plans state specific short- and long-term goals, and if these goals are not reached, reassessment needs to be done to set up new goals. Consultation with client, family, and other significant supports guides the planning and helps the case manager to set up the most realistic, attainable goals (see the case study on p. 108).

Counseling

Basing their interventions on assessments and plans, case managers counsel the client/patient, family, friends, and other involved professionals to help them with issues related to chronic illness, disability, loss of status and finances, environmental problems, family stresses, and so on. They help both clients/patients and their families deal with a range of intense emotions such as anger, resentment, anxiety, guilt, loneliness, sadness, depression, love, and hate. These emotions may have a long history or, on the other hand, may result from the stresses of seemingly intractable new problems identified during the assessment period.

---

*In contrast, nurses sometimes think of assessment as part of a skillfully developed problem list that gives brief *Subjective* and *Objective* observations, followed by a concise *Assessment* and treatment *Plan* (S.O.A.P.). For example, Problem #1: Poor bladder control. *S.* Niece reports Miss O. takes off Pampers (adult diapers), urinates on herself and around the house. *O.* Pampers not working: Need other techniques. *A.* Regular toileting schedule needs to be introduced. *P.* RN will train aide and family to take Miss O. to the toilet at regular intervals during the day.

Referrals

Referrals help implement the treatment care plan by obtaining needed services for elderly clients/patients. There are three main service categories to which frail elderly are referred:

1. General Health Services: hospitals, doctors, specialty nurses, physiotherapists, occupational therapists, speech therapists, aides
2. Community Services: housing organizations, senior centers, adult day care centers, respite centers, cleaning services, self-help groups, meals-on-wheels, religious organizations, transportation services, entitlement programs, nursing homes
3. Specialists: dietitians, specialty social workers, psychotherapists, lawyers

The utilization of these three categories of services by many clients/patients and their families is often achieved only after much skilled counseling, which in turn depends upon a number of preliminary steps. These include investigating the admission criteria of various referral sources, processing many complicated forms, and attending preliminary interviewing visits with and without clients/patients and their families.

Maintaining an Effective Care Plan

Through regular home visits and telephone calls, the case manager maintains the effectiveness of the treatment plan, but this plan is never written in stone. It must periodically be reviewed and, if necessary, altered as the condition of the client/patient either improves or worsens. The multiphased processes of effective care plan maintenance, therefore, include the ongoing obtaining, monitoring, supervising, coordinating, and reassessing of services. Such constant activity keeps a treatment care plan strong and ensures that the most appropriate and economical services are given.

As we have seen in Chapter 3, sometimes professional case managers must act in a filial role as surrogates for adult children who are unable to contribute to this maintenance function due to other overwhelming problems in their lives or because they are geographically distant.

Dealing with Special Needs

Alzheimer's disease and other forms of dementia, hospice work, and extreme physical disability are among the most taxing situations for elderly clients/patients and their families, friends, and aides. Case managers need to maintain especially close contact with clients/patients and their informal and formal supports throughout the radical change of behaviors that often characterize these most difficult cases. Aides need to be particularly well screened and selected for their expertise in handling these severe illnesses and are often given daily supervisory case management support, especially while the care plan is being refined and stabilized. The wandering, incontinence, and agitation of the Alzheimer's disease client/patient, for example, will usually lead to premature nursing home placement unless the family has a strong geriatric case management team to help care for their unfortunate loved one.

Financial Planning

Sometimes many counseling sessions must be held before elderly clients/patients and/or their families can accept such ideas as:

1. "spending down" to the Medicaid level;
2. cost-sharing with nonprofit community agencies to receive aide services;
3. accepting referrals to (a) publicly funded entitlements and programs (Medicare, Medicaid, meals-on-wheels), (b) lawyers, and (c) other financial planners.; and
4. spending money for needed medical specialists.

Out of the trusting case management relationship, it becomes possible to overcome typically destructive patterns of behavior, such as denial, undue pride, pretended penury, the fear of abandonment, and undue suspiciousness. Only then can the financial aspects of long-term care planning progress.

CONTRIBUTORS TO CASE MANAGEMENT

The Client/Patient

A sometimes unrecognized and untapped resource in case management, and the most important resource when clients/patients are competent, is clients/patients themselves who can assume (and have the right to demand) responsibility for obtaining, monitoring, and supervising many of the services provided to them (see the discussion of *protagonismo* in Chapter 6). The vicissitudes of illness make formal professional case management a necessity, but a sensitive partnership and the sharing of case management tasks increase the independence and self-esteem of the client/patient, as well as greatly assisting the professional case manager.

Family Members and Friends

This informal support system provides much of the care for elderly clients/patients. They are often more accessible and able to offer more individualized and idiosyncratic assistance than the formal case managers. Family members and friends provide many material and affective supports, drawing on lifelong patterns of involvement with the client/patient. When not overwhelmed themselves by other family or work responsibilities, and when in good health, they can be facilitators, protectors, advocates, buffers, and intermediaries with bureaucracies, as well as sources of information about concrete entitlements (housing, pensions, medical care, insurance, etc.). Involved family and friends need the help of professional case managers for the development of assessment and treatment care plans and for support and advice when crises occur.

The Master's in Social Work (MSW)

MSWs are trained in a variety of communication skills that enable them to interact empathically with their clients/patients and their families. They are educated to make assessments and plans that take into account the physical, psychological, social, and cultural factors in the lives of their clients. They know how to match resources with the particular case in question. Through their training they become aware of the importance of encouraging empowerment and of establishing productive links between clients and the communities in which they live. Home care MSWs, associated with hospital and free-standing nurse-directed programs in the community, obtain particular skills in the case management of homebound and at-risk elderly through their home-visiting job experiences and through geriatric specialty training. Working in an interdisciplinary manner with MDs and RNs, they often move into some traditional nursing areas.

The Registered Nurse (RN)

Nurses understand the nature and symptomatology of diseases and are licensed by the state to perform numerous therapeutic services. They are knowledgeable about activities of daily living, exercise, and nutrition. They can be authorized to administer medications and have a close working relationship with doctors. Many RNs have specialized education in the psychological aspects of illness. They benefit from not bearing the stigma that the elderly often associate with the need for mental health specialists such as social workers. They may therefore be more easily accepted into an elderly person's home because of this perceived medical "task" orientation. Once they are accepted and trusted RNs can often go on to perform some traditional social work tasks.

Other Graduate and Postgraduate Professionals

These specialists include doctors, private geriatric care managers, and specialists in public health, gerontology, psychology, and special education. Most are in private practice and are available twenty-four hours a day for both telephone calls and home visits and can respond quickly to the client/patient. Some are able to give the client/patient a great deal of attention and provide the maximum in services, since they can control their caseloads and are working with individuals who have adequate financial resources.

Medicaid Case Managers

These governmental case managers have a variety of educational backgrounds and in-service job training. Many are without benefit of graduate training and are overwhelmed by (1) huge caseloads of indigent clients/patients and impoverished formerly middle-class elderly to whom they can presently only offer limited resources, and (2) numerous and changing governmental rules and regulations that are difficult to integrate into daily practice.

It is unfortunate that these difficult working conditions prevent most Medicaid case managers from having in-depth individual involvement with clients/patients. This hinders their ability to provide optimum services.

The Paraprofessional

Home aides have various titles—home attendants, personal care workers, home health aides, homemakers, home managers, etc. They also have various job descriptions and uneven levels of training. They have more daily contact with clients/patients than any other representative of the formal home care system. They are a critical force in maintaining clients/patients safely at home, yet they are frequently undervalued and exploited.

Home aides often come from diverse cultures. For example, in New York City most paraprofessional aides are from black and Hispanic cultures, with origins in the West Indies, the American South, Central America, and Africa. When given the opportunity, this paraprofessional can bring new creative ideas from his or her culture to enrich the work. With appropriate supervision, training, salaries, and benefits, and when treated with the respect they deserve by clients/patients, families, and the agencies that employ them, these paraprofessionals can transmit the resultant increased competence and self-esteem into optimum care for their elderly clients/patients.

Another helpful paraprofessional group is the home care agency's administrative staff. This staff receives the initial calls from potential clients/patients as well as calls from family members and aides. They frequently provide ventilation opportunities, reassurances, financial and scheduling information, information on community resources, and a telephone socializing outlet for home-bound elderly.

CASE STUDY ILLUSTRATING ASPECTS
OF SKILLED CASE MANAGEMENT

Identifying Information

Mrs. Collins is an alert, intelligent, very frail eighty-five-year-old who was widowed two years ago. She lives alone in a third-floor walk-up studio apartment, located on a tenement block within a mainly affluent urban neighborhood. Mrs. Collins has lived her entire life on this block. She and her devoted husband had been the superintendents of a small apartment house across the street from where she now lives. They both attended services at the Catholic church up the block, and shopped in the next-door grocery store. Mrs. C. has always been very strong-willed, hardworking, and independent and today proudly calls herself a "loner." Mr. and Mrs. Collins never had children; her only sister is dead, but she receives calls and visits from her two married nieces, who live seventy-five miles away.

Three months ago, Mrs. Collins began rejecting the calls and visits of her nieces. Neighbors had observed that her tendency to withdraw began with her husband's death. She stopped going to church, refused church visits and calls, went out shopping only once a week, and stayed inside the rest of the time. One concerned neighbor alerted a community social service agency that assigned a social worker, who made a home visit. Mrs. Collins refused to open the door, saying that she was well and had a right to her privacy. The agency maintained weekly telephone contact, much to Mrs. Collins' displeasure.

Precipitating Event

Mrs. Collins fell in her home. Her neighbor heard cries of pain and called the superintendent, who opened the unclean apartment, found Mrs. Collins on the floor, and called 911. During hospitalization, Mrs. Collins was diagnosed as having congestive heart failure (CHF), and a fractured shoulder as a result of her fall. It was the foot and leg edema associated with CHF that hindered her walking ability, leading to the fall. Mrs. Collins was well cared for in the hospital. Her community social worker maintained regular telephone contact, which was now gratefully accepted. Her edema was reduced by medications. The hospital social worker, at the time of discharge, contacted the hospital's home care department, which provided a visiting nurse and physiotherapist paid for by Medicare. Medications were prescribed and ambulette services arranged, but because Mrs. Collins was now ambulating well, Medicare would not pay for any aide services. The social worker from the community agency, learning of the hospitalization and discharge with no home aide, informed the hospital social worker of Mrs. Collins' past isolated social history and the need for some hours of aide services. Both workers learned from the nieces that Mrs. Collins had adequate savings, and with a mighty effort from all concerned professionals and the nieces, Mrs. Collins accepted an aide from COHME on a private-pay basis.

Initial Assessment

Mrs. Collins is reactively depressed following the death of her husband two years ago. Childless, with minimal family involvement and facing multiple losses (the death of her devoted husband, retirement from work, heart disease, aging, and the recent effects of malnutrition), she continues to struggle to maintain as much independence as possible. It appears unlikely that Mrs. Collins, given her past "loner" lifestyle, will greatly change her behavior; however, fear of the possibility of another fall has allowed her to accept the placement of an aide, and she sees that the quality of her life has already somewhat improved. If the aide remains sensitive to Mrs. Collins' need to do as much as possible for herself, Mrs. Collins may accept her permanently. Ongoing supportive case management of concrete issues important to Mrs. Collins, as enumerated in the following plan, will probably be accepted.

Plan

1. Maintain weekly case management involvement.
2. Consider future psychiatric assessment.
3. Consider involvement in a senior group.

4. Consider more involvement from family and friends.
5. Place and support an aide four hours, five days per week to:
   (a) be a companion; (b) encourage Mrs. Collins to go out;
   (c) shop; (d) help with cooking; (e) do laundry; (f) do light
   housekeeping; (g) monitor medications; (h) monitor nutritional status; and (i) observe legs for edema.

One Year Later

Mrs. Collins likes and has totally accepted the Jamaican aide
assigned to her. The aide cooks "Island" food with her (limiting the
salt and spices), and brings her own granddaughter to visit occasionally. These two very positive additions to Mrs. Collins' support
network have exposed Mrs. Collins to a new culture, increased her
interest in eating and in trying new foods, and given her companions
she pays and, therefore, controls to some extent, unlike the situation
with her family. While recuperating, she accepted COHME's RN and
MSW case management monthly visits for four months then strongly
rejected both, since their treatment planning goals conflicted with her
own. She now tolerates weekly telephone calls from the community
social worker. Depression has been replaced by anger and mild
suspiciousness toward any new professional. She sees her old MD
and makes needed medical plan changes when encouraged to do so
by her aide, who then reports any physical changes to COHME. The
COHME RN assesses the aide's oral report over the phone and
instructs the aide. The RN calls Mrs. Collins' doctor if the aide
reports unusual changes.

Mrs. Collins has developed a positive, strong telephone relationship with COHME's administrative assistant, whom she calls weekly to discuss her bill. This seems to be a kind of telephone reassur-
ance on her part and on her terms. These business calls enable her to
maintain a sense of control over her life.

Results

Mrs. Collins' depression has ended. She is accepting the aide,
seeing her MD regularly, taking her medications regularly, and
eating regularly with good weight gain. Her appearance has im-

proved, and her living environment has been upgraded with the addition of a new sink and reclining chair. Several reassessments by the MSW and RN over the year have indicated that many items of the original care plan are presently unneeded or unaccepted by the client/patient. The client/patient is doing well at home.

CONTROVERSIES
IN THE CASE MANAGEMENT FIELD

The steadily increasing size of the elderly population in the United States has led to current projections that by the year 2050 a quarter of our population will be over the age of sixty-five. Obviously, such a development will require ever more comprehensive and varied services to meet the needs of this rapidly growing elderly population. At the same time, however, although there is a fairly widespread recognition of the importance of this phenomenon, there is no unanimity about ways and means of dealing with it. The fact that case management is done by people coming from many different disciplines complicates the issue even more. Several of the controversies that have arisen in recent years concerning the relationship between case management and the changing demographic structure of the United States are briefly summarized here:

1. With respect to the public service sector, many people fear that governmental funding agencies are trying to save money by employing workers with limited case management training. It is felt that these less costly workers, who perform limited concrete services, do not really meet client/patient psychological needs. It is also felt that these workers are overworked and undertrained. Some critics feel that a prevalent "administrative perspective" permeates large public agencies and overlooks the human needs of dependent elderly.
2. In agencies that employ well-trained MSW case managers, the same "administrative perspective" is thought to sacrifice the full use of valuable professional skills such as counseling because of the need to process heavy caseloads and because of various agency constraints such as hospital diagnostic-related groups (DRGs) and managed care.

3. The title "case manager" offends many of the very individuals who hold it. They resent the fact that their elderly clients/ patients are called "cases" and resent the bureaucratic assumption that just because an elderly person lacks money and is placed on Medicaid, for example, he or she needs to have his or her whole life supervised.

4. The social work profession has asked for clarification about the various disciplines that perform case management services. The profession of social work worries that its members, some of whom have become part of a new specialty (i.e., profit-making private geriatric care management [PGCM]), may be shifting away from traditional social work values. These values call for treatment of the needy within an agency setting, in which social workers receive a modest salary. PGCM people work privately, appear to have fewer pressures, charge what critics feel are exorbitant fees, welcome into their ranks people from disciplines other than social work (RNs, psychologists, etc.), usually treat only clients/patients who can afford their fees, and appear to have higher status than the traditional agency social worker. Some traditional social workers fear the onset of a separate, two-tiered case management service system—one for the rich, and one for the poor—as PGCM continues its development. Some public service social workers also worry that PGCM people, by helping only wealthier clients/patients, are leaving those with more problems and fewer resources to the already overburdened public sector.

PGCM people counter that they refer the elderly who cannot afford them to public agencies, thereby increasing the latter's censuses and funding base. They maintain that their fees are not high when their separate overhead expenses are considered, and indeed feel that if agency social workers costed out their funded services, PGCM fees might be equal or even less. Also, their middle-class clients/patients are ineligible to receive services from many nonprofit agencies. PGCM workers maintain that as independent practitioners they have different but equally difficult administrative problems and stresses to handle as do agency practitioners. PGCM people experience long waiting periods to receive referrals, face the unpredictability of income, and have the extra expenses of setting up an entrepreneurial practice. Their twenty-four hour availability, some report, is only compensated for by their freedom from agency constraints and the possibility of doing optimum care management.

NEW DIRECTIONS

Medicaid home attendants, who provide many case management services for their poor clients, and who used to receive only the minimum wage, are now getting higher salaries and some health insurance benefits in New York City. This increase in pay and benefits reflects a higher level of governmental awareness of just how important these paraprofessional aides are; it may help to keep more experienced workers in the field.

Large business corporations, wanting to cut down the enormous cost of employee absenteeism, are setting up contracts with a variety of governmental, voluntary, and private case managers. These companies want to help valued employees who are frequently away from work providing care to chronically ill, often elderly family members, while at the same time lessening health costs for the company.

It is unclear whether these and some other positive new directions in home care will develop into a significant trend. Public agencies, pessimistic about future government financial support, are beginning to consider the possibility of becoming "partners in care" with private case managers and of accepting middle-class clients for pay. Hard economic times pave the way for creative planning and new political partnerships.

COHME's cooperative emphasis makes it easier for all participants in case management to work together on the plan while continuing to recognize the specific expertise of social work in the overall assessment and coordination roles.

Chapter 12

Teaching the Uses
of the COHME One-Sheet

In November 1992, I spoke at the Rockefeller College Institute
on Case Management about COHME's One-Sheet. My audience
consisted of Medicaid caseworkers (some with and some without
BSWs) struggling to do case management within the framework of
a large governmental agency with shrinking resources. I was concerned that they might find information about our small agency,
COHME, rather reminiscent of a social work Fantasyland. I was
reminded of the tensions I had noted at the meetings between city-
employed social workers and the cooperative CADIAI aides in
Bologna (see Chapter 6). Fortunately, they found the presentation
most useful.

PRESENTATION

Everyone with COHME performs some case management tasks:
the receptionist, the bookkeeper, the office manager, the home
aides, the nurses, the social workers, the families of clients, significant other formal and informal contacts and, of course, whenever
possible, our clients. It would be impossible, however, to handle the
massive amount of input we receive from all these concerned
people without a focal point, a person to collect and coordinate the
case management material. We've developed the function and title
of Case Management Team Coordinator (CMTC), which is held
only by our MSWs. The CMTCs pull together oral and written
information received from all the other participants in the case

management process, make assessments and plans, and change, modify, and/or improve the original treatment plan on a weekly basis.

The original treatment plan is developed from information obtained during the first in-person contact, either at home or in the hospital. For each case, *and for each home visit*, we use a unique One-Sheet method of recording the precipitating event, identifying information, assessment, and plan. We never write more than that one sheet. Why? Because we want that sheet to be read and used. Long psychosocial assessments, we've learned from sad experience, really aren't read, used, or needed at COHME. We train our CMTCs to be concise and accurate. We were very influenced by the concise S.O.A.P. plans used by RNs, which I discussed in a manual written for Medicaid workers in Indiana (see Chapter 11). We stress the fact that without this brief One-Sheet assessment, we cannot give good home care to our clients. We tell our CMTCs that their work, carefully conceptualized in the One-Sheet, gives the agency the reason for being. Without the CMTC insights, assessments, and plans, no one else can function at COHME. Figure 12.1 is an example of a well-used One-Sheet, which I'll go over with you now.

Well, you might say, the material presented in this One-Sheet is fine for COHME, but case managers in a Medicaid agency function quite differently from CMTCs at COHME. Yet, is that really true?

As some have said, we are a model for case management, a "living laboratory," if you will. Most of you probably think you're too harried with your huge caseloads to do case management the way we do it. If you agree with my premise that social work case management is the core of home care, and you've come here to get new ideas for your practice, I'd like to give you an example of Medicaid case managers who were taught our method very successfully under conditions like yours.

I taught COHME's case management One-Sheet method at a senior housing center in a poor Hispanic community in East Harlem for twenty-six sessions over a one-year period, 1988 to 1989. The case managers were all dedicated workers, exhausted from running around trying to get Medicaid for all their clients. All the social workers and administrators were together in one large, undivided room. Clients ran in and out, phones rang all the time, workers called to one another, the

FIGURE 12.1. COHME One-Sheet

COHME One-Sheet   6/1/92   Client: Mrs. Dee, 82   CMTC HV#4

PRECIPITATING EVENT: "Invasion" of Mrs. Dee's apartment last night by police.

IDENTIFYING INFORMATION: Honey, Mrs. Dee's aide, called me shortly after she arrived at work, saying Mrs. Dee was crying and trembling about the "invasion." Mrs. Dee agreed to my immediate home visit. When I arrived at Mrs. Dee's lobby, her intercom didn't work. I got into the apartment when another tenant came with a key. Mrs. Dee had no night aide coverage and didn't call the COHME coverage RN when the crisis occurred. Since early this morning, Honey and the super's wife, Anita, had been in Mrs. Dee's very worn, clean, small studio apartment, comforting her. Mrs. Dee now appeared calm and didn't want to discuss the trauma with me. Mrs. Dee's window gate was loose, caused last night, Honey said, by police entering her apt. when she didn't answer their knock, because of her deafness. The police had been called by Mrs. Dee's cousin, Sara, when Mrs. Dee didn't answer the phone. Anita was arranging to have the gate fixed today, and at my suggestion will also have the intercom fixed. Although Mrs. Dee was wearing her hearing aids, we still had to communicate mostly through my shouting, gesturing, and writing. Mrs. Dee quietly stated she'd now accept the audiologist I'd previously suggested, then spoke of her need for hearing aid batteries, light bulbs, and a garter belt. Honey stated she'd buy these items today, along with bathroom equipment we'd also previously suggested. Honey reported Sara wanted Mrs. Dee to come live near her in North Carolina. Mrs. Dee screamed: "She's crazy by the nubs! This is my home and I want to stay here, whatever happens." I said I wanted her to stay at home, too. She nodded, but still refused to further discuss her feelings about the invasion with me. She will allow me to call Sara. She then raised several financial concerns, which we'd already been working on for two weeks. Mrs. Dee then called me over and kissed my cheek. We arranged a visit for next week.

ASSESSMENT: Mrs. Dee refused to directly discuss last night's trauma with me, since she didn't completely trust me. She feared I might somehow make her leave her beloved home. A fiercely independent woman, struggling mightily against growing dependency, she previously identified me as the "snoopy" social worker. She had discussed only her practical problems with me, rejecting most of my ideas. The crisis provided an opportunity for me to gain her trust, and assure her that I wanted her to be safe at home. Now she trusts me and we can complete our plans. She uses her excellent informal support group and aide to ventilate her appropriate anxieties and do concrete tasks for her, but she begins to see I have other expertises that can help her. Her cousin overreacted, unaware of Mrs. Dee's increasing deafness and also unaware of how strong her support system is in the building. Better communication with family is needed.

PLAN: (1) Call cousin Sara; bring her up to date, especially re: Mrs. Dee's excellent support system, her increasing deafness, and our plans. (2) Continue care plan from three previous visits, adding audiologist appointment and possible church involvement. (3) Be sure super makes agreed-upon repairs.

radio played, everyone got along well, and a lot of work got done! One social worker, Maritza, said to me as I marveled at the flurry of activity: "Our clients don't think we're doing anything for them unless we are running around here, or at Medicaid, getting them an aide."

We began our work together by my trying to adjust to their supercharged, noisy work environment. The energy was wonderful!

We started with the most difficult cases. Indeed, all social work plans included going down to Medicaid for an aide, as Maritza had previously mentioned. As I tried to pin Maritza and the others down on an assessment, sometimes after months of work with a client, I realized they had none. They did what the client and family wanted. As they told me the complexities of a given case, I could not hold all their ideas in my head with all the other activities that were going on. I asked the administrator if I could have a private room for our meetings, but there was none; however, the next week, the room hushed when I came in, the phone bells were turned off, and the social workers were freed from other tasks during my teaching visit. We got down to hard work, concentrating on the COHME One-Sheet model: precipitating event, identifying information, assessment, and plan. You might think these workers needed to have an MSW to do this. No, the One-Sheet material is so specific that a caseworker under MSW supervision can be taught to do it. In fact, the caseworkers I taught added their own interpretations:

- *Precipitating event* meant: "Why I'm involved now."
- *Identifying information* meant: "I'm telling an objective story. I just want the facts, Ma'am."
- *Assessment* meant: "What I professionally think is happening and what needs to be done."
- *Plan* meant: "Exactly what I'm going to do."

By session twelve, the caseworkers were making assessments and plans without me, but they were making them too swiftly. We took note of the many useless hours still spent running around, trying to provide services for clients that turned out to be wrong, unnecessary, or inappropriate.

Time, reflective time, must be spent preparing a thoughtful, well-formulated assessment. So during this crucial twelfth session, we re-worked an old assessment that had previously led to a plan requiring at least ten hours of nonproductive "running around," as they themselves described it. The caseworkers produced all the new ideas for the reworked assessment. They just had to give it their concentrated attention. They said to me at the end of this particularly productive session: "I guess if you don't think with your head, you have to think with your feet!"

"Gee," I said, "that's what my mom always told me. Some wisdom transcends age and cultural orientation, right?"

Imagine everyone's surprise when they discovered that getting Medicaid and an aide was not the answer in many of their most difficult cases. Families needed to be shown how to access the most appropriate help. Other community agencies were available—all the workers had to do was pick up the phone and make a referral to them. Sometimes it was necessary to replace an unresponsive MD. In one case a new MD changed the medications for a frail, homebound, elderly client who soon felt so much better that he no longer needed an aide.

Another avenue to be explored was the formal and informal networks available to the client. Often there was a senior center near the client and a willing relative who could provide some support.

I must repeat that quiet, reflective time is always needed to develop the One-Sheet. I sometimes feel the best thing I did in my teaching at this senior housing center was to validate the need for a part-time social work office with a door that closed for the caseworkers to use—just for developing the One-Sheet. One caseworker I taught in East Harlem said that we were helping our clients to "get a life of their own." Maybe we social workers need to "get a room of our own."

CONCLUDING THOUGHTS

A colleague called me recently at work. We had a stimulating discussion about a provocative administrative home care conference we had both attended. She then asked me pointedly how I knew when COHME was functioning well.

I answered that I knew COHME was functioning well when the lack of office-related stress allowed me to have the kind of thoughtful conversation I was having with her at that moment.

Of course, as with virtually every organization, COHME still has occasional difficult and stressful moments. Geriatric social work practice and the development of cooperative strategies present new challenges as staff and regulations change. But I believe COHME's struggle to resolve these stresses and challenges is critical for our profession at this time.

We have been fortunate to have a "living laboratory" at COHME, which has allowed us to test what works and does not work in traditional social work practice and to determine what should be introduced, changed, or adapted to fit new home health care needs.

The One-Sheet presents geriatric social work practice in a manner that makes clear its primacy in comprehensive case management, a subject under dispute within our government today. Through cooperative strategies social workers can ensure that they have the collegial support that helps prevent burnout.

We must, however, be more assertive on behalf of ourselves and our profession, and assume our share of responsibility and power as case management team coordinators in geriatric home health care. Our clients, their families, and our co-workers deserve no less.

Index